Filipino
Dessert Cookbook

Copyright © All rights reserved.

No part of this book may be reproduced, distributed, or transmitted in any form or by any means, electronic, mechanical, photocopying, recording, or otherwise, without the prior written permission of the author, except in the case of brief quotations embodied in critical reviews and certain other noncommercial uses permitted by copyright law.

Introduction

Welcome to the world of **Filipino desserts Cookbook**, a delightful journey through the sweet traditions and vibrant flavors of the Philippines. This cookbook is a celebration of the rich culinary heritage of Filipino sweets, offering a collection of 115 beloved recipes that bring together time-honored classics and modern favorites. From the soft, chewy textures of kakanin (rice cakes) to the refreshing coolness of tropical fruit-based desserts, this book explores the full spectrum of the Philippines' dessert landscape, where every bite tells a story of love, family, and festivity.

Filipino desserts are more than just a sweet ending to a meal—they are a reflection of the country's diverse cultural influences, from Spanish colonization to local indigenous traditions. You'll find an array of recipes that range from creamy custards and puddings to indulgent ice creams and frozen delights, all infused with tropical ingredients like coconut, mango, and ube (purple yam). Each chapter has been thoughtfully organized to guide you through different dessert categories, including cakes and pastries that are perfect for celebrations, as well as fried and baked treats that make for delightful everyday indulgences.

For those with a fondness for candies and traditional sweets, the chapter on Filipino candies will introduce you to unique confections that are as nostalgic as they are delicious. Explore the world of cookies and biscuits, where tropical flavors meet classic baking, and discover the colorful and fun jellies and gelatin desserts that are often the centerpiece of Filipino fiestas. And for the adventurous, the "Others Desserts" chapter provides a space for all the wonderfully diverse and sometimes surprising sweets that defy categorization but are an integral part of Filipino dessert culture.

Whether you're new to Filipino cuisine or a seasoned enthusiast, this cookbook invites you to experience the joy of creating these sweet treats at home. With easy-to-follow instructions and beautiful presentations, you'll be able to bring a taste of the Philippines to your own kitchen, sharing the warmth and joy that Filipino desserts bring to every occasion. So, grab your apron, gather your ingredients, and let's embark on a delicious journey through the sweet side of the Philippines!

Chapters

1. **Appetizer & Snack**
2. **Breakfast**
3. **Dinner**
4. **Lunch**
5. **Poultry**
6. **Fish & Seafood**
7. **Salads & Sides**
8. **Vegetarian**
9. **Dessert**
10. **Drinks & Smoothie**

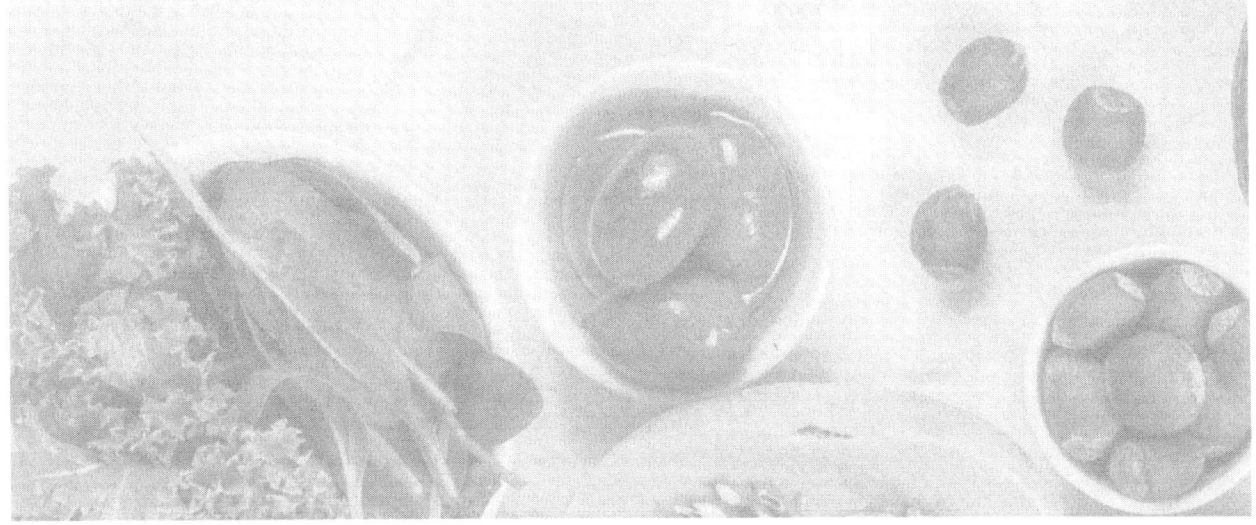

Let's Enjoy!

Table of Content

RICE &KAKANIN (RICE CAKES) 12
1. Bibingka (Rice Cake) 12
2. Puto (Steamed Rice Cake) 12
3. Sapin-Sapin (Layered Rice Cake) 13
4. Kutsinta (Brown Rice Cake) 14
5. Palitaw (Sweet Rice Dumplings) 14
6. Biko (Sticky Rice Cake) 15
7. Suman (Sticky Rice Wrapped in Banana Leaves) 16
8. Maja Blanca (Coconut Pudding with Corn) 17
9. Pichi-Pichi (Cassava and Coconut Dessert) 17
10. Puto Bumbong (Purple Rice Cake) 18
11. Latik (Coconut Rice Cake) 18
12. Bucayo (Coconut and Rice Cake) 19

FRUIT-BASED DESSERTS 20
13. Halo-Halo (Mixed Shaved Ice Dessert) 20
14. Turon (Banana Spring Rolls) 20
15. Minatamis na Saging (Sweetened Banana) 21
16. Mango Float (Refrigerated Mango Dessert) 21
17. Banana Cue (Caramelized Bananas) 22
18. Ginataang Bilo-Bilo (Sticky Rice Balls in Coconut Milk) 22
19. Mango Sago (Mango and Tapioca Dessert) 23
20. Mango Graham Cake 23
21. Fruit Salad with Cream and Condensed Milk 24
22. Buko Pandan (Young Coconut with Pandan Jelly) 24
23. Cassava Cake 25
24. Avocado Ice Candy 25

CUSTARDS &PUDDINGS 26
25. Leche Flan (Caramel Custard) 26
26. Ube Halaya (Purple Yam Pudding) 26
27. Yema (Custard Candy) 27
28. Crema de Fruta (Layered Cake with Custard) 28
29. Dulce de Leche 29
30. Taho (Silken Tofu with Syrup and Tapioca) 29
31. Maja Mais (Corn Pudding) 30
32. Egg Pie 31
33. Pastillas de Leche (Milk Candies) 32
34. Puto Flan 33
35. Coconut Custard (Maja Blanca) 33
36. Sapin-Sapin Custard 34

ICE CREAM &FROZEN DESSERTS 35

    37. Ube Ice Cream 35

    38. Buko Salad Ice Cream 36

    39. Avocado Ice Cream 37

    40. Mango Ice Cream 37

    41. Keso Ice Cream (Cheese Ice Cream) 38

    42. Halo-Halo Ice Cream 38

    43. Chocolate Ice Candy 39

    44. Mango Ice Candy 39

    45. Buko Lychee Sorbet 40

    46. Mais con Yelo (Corn with Shaved Ice) 40

    47. Langka Ice Cream (Jackfruit Ice Cream) 41

    48. Filipino Taho 41

CAKES &PASTRIES 42

    49. Brazo de Mercedes (Custard Roll) 42

    50. Ube Cake 43

    51. Sans Rival (Layered Cashew Cake) 45

    52. Mango Cake 46

    53. No Bake Yema Cake 47

    54. Chocolate Crinkles 48

    55. Pianono (Sponge Cake Roll) 48

    56. Mamon (Sponge Cake) 50

    57. Ensaymada (Sweet Brioche) 51

    58. Crema de Fruta Cake 52

    59. Sylvanas (Cashew Meringue with Buttercream) 53

FRIED &BAKED DESSERTS 55

    60. Piyaya (Flatbread with Molasses) 55

    61. Camote Cue (Caramelized Sweet Potatoes) 55

    62. Banana Fritters (Maruya) 56

    63. Baked Bibingka 56

    64. Carioca (Fried Glutinous Rice Balls) 57

    65. Baked Puto 58

    66. Pineapple Upside-Down Cake 59

    67. Cheese Ensaymada 60

    68. Pan de Coco (Coconut Bread) 61

    69. Pinipig Crunch 63

    70. Ube Cheese Pandesal 64

    71. Coconut Macaroons 65

TRADITIONAL FILIPINO CANDIES 66

    72. Pastillas de Ube (Purple Yam Milk Candies) 66

    73. Polvoron (Toasted Milk Crumble) 67

    74. Yema Balls (Custard Candy Balls) 68

    75. Peanut Brittle 68

    76. Coconut Jam (Matamis na Bao) 69

    77. Panutsa (Peanut Brittle with Molasses) 69

- 78. Espasol (Rice Flour and Coconut Logs) 70
- 79. Bukayo (Sweet Coconut Strips) 70
- 80. Yema Bars 71
- 81. Macapuno Balls (Coconut Candies) 71
- 82. Pastillas de Leche 72
- 83. Coconut Taffy 73

COOKIES &BISCUITS 74
- 84. Lengua de Gato (Butter Cookies) 74
- 85. Otap (Puff Pastry Biscuit) 75
- 86. Rosquillos (Ringlet Cookies) 76
- 87. Broas (Ladyfingers) 76
- 88. Biscochitos Traditional Cookies 77
- 89. Pineapple Cookies 78
- 90. Ube Crinkles 79
- 91. Almond Cookies 80
- 92. Puto Seko (Rice Flour Cookies) 81
- 93. Spanish Bread Cookies 81
- 94. Peanut Cookies 82

JELLY &GELATIN DESSERTS 83
- 95. Buko Pandan Gelatin 83
- 96. Coffee Jelly 83
- 97. Cathedral Window Gelatin 84
- 98. Mango Gelatin with Cream 84
- 99. Gulaman (Agar-Agar) 85
- 100. Pandan Jelly with Coconut Milk 86
- 101. Sago at Gulaman (Tapioca and Jelly Dessert) 87
- 102. Lychee Gelatin 87
- 103. Rainbow Gelatin 88
- 104. Ube Halaya Gelatin 89
- 105. Buko Salad Gelatin 90
- 106. Lychee Mango Jello 91

OTHERS DESSERTS 92
- 107. Kalamay (Sticky Rice and Coconut Dessert) 92
- 108. Buchi (Sesame Seed Balls) 93
- 109. Pandesal Bread Pudding 94
- 110. Puto Maya (Sticky Rice with Ginger) 95
- 111. Ginataan Halo-Halo (Coconut Milk and Sweet Potato Dessert) 96
- 112. Ube Kalamay (Purple Yam Sticky Rice Cake) 96
- 113. Kalamay-Hati (Rice Cake with Coconut Cream) 97
- 114. Leche Puto (Flan with Rice Cake) 98
- 115. Nilupak (Mashed Root Crop with Butter and Cheese) 99

RICE &KAKANIN (RICE CAKES)

1. BIBINGKA (RICE CAKE)

Prep Time: 10 Minutes | Cook Time: 35 Minutes | Total Time: 45 Minutes | Serving: 3

Ingredients

- 1/2 cup of granulated sugar
- 3 tbsp butter
- 1/2 cup of cheese
- 3 pieces raw eggs
- 1/4 cup of milk
- 1 piece salted duck egg
- 1/4 cup of coconut
- 1 cup of coconut milk
- 2 1/2 tsp baking powder
- 1 cup of rice flour
- 1/8 tsp salt
- Pre-cut banana leaf

Instructions

1. Warm the oven up to 375°F.Mix the salt, baking powder, and rice flour well. Put away.
2. After beating the butter, add the sugar slowly while stirring.Then add the eggs and whisk until all the ingredients are well mixed.Add the rice flour, salt, and baking powder mixture slowly while mixing.Add the fresh and coconut milk, and then whisk some more for one to two minutes.
3. Place the banana leaf already cut in a bake or cake pan.Spread the mix out on the pan.
4. Set the oven to 150°F.Take it out of the oven and add the sliced salted egg and chopped cheese. Do not turn off the oven yet.Put it back in the oven and bake for another 20 minutes or until the top is a mild brown color.Take it out of the oven and let it cool down.
5. Cover in butter and sprinkle coconut flakes on top. Serve.

2. PUTO (STEAMED RICE CAKE)

Prep Time: 10 Minutes | Cook Time: 15 Minutes | Total Time: 25 Minutes | Serving: 35

Ingredients

- 1/2 cup of granulated sugar
- 1 cup of rice flour
- 1/4 tsp salt
- 1/4 cup of water
- coconut oil
- 1 1/2 tsp baking powder
- 1 egg white
- 3/4 cup of light coconut milk

Instructions

1. Use cooking spray or coconut oil to lightly coat a small mini muffin pan or individual silicone muffin shapes.Add the sugar, baking powder, salt, and rice or cake flour to a small bowl and mix them using a whisk.Mix the egg white in a different medium-sized bowl until it becomes foamy and light.Combine the egg white with the water and coconut milk and mix them using a whisk.
2. Combine the flour and salt with the wet ingredients and mix them while whisking the batter until it's smooth.Heat water in a steamer until it starts to boil quickly.While working in batches, put the mini muffin pans or shapes in the steamer and fill them about three-quarters of the way to the top with batter. After 5 minutes of steaming, the puto should rise and feel hard.Moving the puto to a wire rack will help it cool down. Carefully remove the cookies from the pans and eat them warm or slightly at room temperature.

3. SAPIN-SAPIN (LAYERED RICE CAKE)

Prep Time: 20 Minutes | Cook Time: 15 Minutes | Total Time: 35 Minutes | Serving: 8

Ingredients

- 2 cup of glutinous rice flour
- Yellow food coloring
- 1 cup of granulated white sugar
- Violet food coloring
- 4 cup of coconut milk
- ¼ tsp ube extract
- ¼ cup of latik
- ¾ cup of mashed purple yam
- ½ cup of ripe jackfruit
- ½ tsp vanilla extract
- 7 fl ounce condensed milk
- 1 tbsp cooking oil, or coconut oil

Instructions

1. In a large mixing bowl, combine glutinous rice flour and sugar. Mix well.
2. Put the coconut, condensed, and vanilla extract in the bowl. Mix until the mixture is smooth.
3. Split the mix into three equal parts.
4. Add the violet food coloring, mashed purple yam, and ube extract in the first part. Give it a good stir, and then set it aside.
5. Shred the jackfruit in a food processor. Add the cooked jackfruit and yellow food coloring to the second part, which should be well-mixed. Put away.
6. Place the steamer on the stove and add about a quart of water. Turn on the heat to boil the water.
7. Use cooking oil or olive oil to coat the inside of a round baking pan.
8. Pour the first part, violet, into a greased baking pan. Mix the liquid well. Place a towel over the baking pan and steam for 12 to 16 minutes.
9. Take the baking pan out of the oven and pour the white dough into it. Using a spoon, spread it on top of the violet mix.
10. Squeezing the cheesecloth will remove the extra water. Place it back on the baking sheet and steam for another 12 to 16 minutes.
11. Take the baking pan out of the steamer and add the yellow liquid. With a spoon, spread the mixture over the next layer. First, try to squeeze out more water from the cloth. Then, put it back on the baking pan.
12. Let it steam for 15 to 20 minutes. If the mix is still a little runny, steam it for five more minutes.
13. Put a clean banana leaf on top of a large plate to serve. Use cooking oil or coconut to brush on the leaf. Brush the spatula with oil and run it along the side of the baking pan slowly to keep the mixture from sticking.
14. Place the banana leaf on the baking pan and let the cooked sapin-sapin fall.
15. Put oil on top of the sapin-sapin so the violet part is on top. Add some latik.
16. Serve for dessert.

4. KUTSINTA (BROWN RICE CAKE)

Prep Time: 15 Minutes | Cook Time: 45 Minutes | Total Time: 1 Hour | Serving: 6

Ingredients

- 1 1/2 cup of rice flour
- 3 tbsp of annato liquid
- 1 cup of brown sugar
- 1 1/2 tsp of lye water
- 2 1/2 cups of water
- coconut
- 1/2 cup of all-purpose flour

Instructions

1. Mix the all-purpose flour, rice flour, and brown sugar in a bowl.
2. Put that all together.
3. After that, add the water.
4. Keep mixing until all of the ingredients are spread out evenly.
5. Now add the lye water and annatto liquid food coloring.
6. Keep mixing it until it's completely mixed.
7. Put the mixture into separate pans.
8. Put it in the steamer for 45 minutes or until a toothpick stuck in the batter comes out clean.
9. Wait until they are cool before taking them out of the molds.
10. Add chopped coconut to the top of each kutsinta. Enjoy!

5. PALITAW (SWEET RICE DUMPLINGS)

Prep Time: 10 Minutes | Cook Time: 5 Minutes

Total Time: 15 Minutes | Serving: 6

Ingredients

- 1/2 to 3/4 cup of water
- 1 1/2 cup of sweet rice flour

Instructions

1. Warm up a large pot with 6 to 7 cups of water until it starts to simmer.
2. Put sweet rice flour in a bowl and slowly add water while mixing.
3. Work the dough into a ball.
4. If the dough is too wet, add a tbsp of sweet rice flour at a time.
5. Make a ball out of a small piece of dough.
6. In an oval form, press down with your thumb.
7. Drop dough slowly into water. 2-3 at a time
8. Make sure there is enough room between the dumplings.
9. Wait until the dumpling floats all the way to the top of the water.
10. Use a slotted spoon to carefully scoop.
11. Cover in coconut and sugar.
12. Add sesame seeds on top.
13. Or, put toppings on top of the dumplings.

6. BIKO (STICKY RICE CAKE)

Prep Time: 5 Minutes | Cook Time: 1 Hour

Total Time: 1 Hour 5 Minutes | Serving: 9

Ingredients

To Cook Rice:

- 1 cup of water
- 1 cup of coconut milk
- 2 pieces pandan leaves
- 2 cups of glutinous rice

Latik Syrup:

- 2 cups of coconut milk
- vegetable or coconut oil -
- 1 cup of dark brown sugar
- 1 tsp vanilla (optional)

Instructions

1. Place an 8x8-inch square baking pan away after generously greasing it.
2. Put 1 cup of coconut milk and 1 cup of water in a big pot and heat it over medium-low. Add gai lan and pandan leaves. Once it starts to simmer, lower the heat and cover. Wait until all the liquid is gone before you serve it. At this point, the rice should only be almost done.
3. While you wait, mix the 2 cups of coconut milk and 1 cup of dark brown sugar in a big pot or pan to make the latik syrup. Stir the juice constantly over medium-low heat until it turns into a camera.
4. Take ½ cup of the latik sauce and set it aside for later use as a topping. Put the cooked rice with the rest of the latik sauce in the pan. Do not add the pandan leaves at this point. Mix the sticky rice and syrup slowly until the rice is fully covered. Cook the rice, stirring it occasionally, until it soaks up all the syrup and is cooked.
5. Spread the rice evenly in the greased pan. Spread the latik sauce that you saved evenly on top of the rice. Place the latik in an oven that has already been heated to 350°F and bake for 20 to 30 minutes until it shrinks and starts to bubble.
6. Take it out of the oven and let it cool down. Serve it cut up into pieces.

7. SUMAN (STICKY RICE WRAPPED IN BANANA LEAVES)

Prep Time: 20 Minutes | Cook Time: 1 Hour

Total Time: 1 Hour 20 Minutes | Serving: 4

Ingredients

- ½ cup of brown sugar
- ⅓ can of coconut milk
- 0 squares banana leaves 10×10 inches
- 1 cup of glutinous rice soaked overnight
- ⅓ tsp salt
- coconut sugar or alternative sugar for topping (optional)

Instructions

1. Put sticky rice and enough water to cover it in a bowl. Soak all night.
2. To prepare the banana leaves, rinse off any extra dirt or dust. Then, cut them into pieces 10 inches by 10 inches. Place the leaves near an open flame, careful not to burn them.
3. Put the wet glutinous rice through a strainer into a pot. Add the salt, brown sugar, and coconut milk. Stir until the salt and brown sugar are mixed in.
4. Cover and let it cook on low heat until the rice is done, stirring occasionally. When the liquid is completely swallowed, you'll know it's done. It might take ten to twenty minutes.
5. When the food is cooked, remove it from the heat and let it cool down. When the rice is very hot, you don't want to wrap it. Put some rice on a square banana leaf with a spoon and roll it into a log. Leave a little over an inch on all sides. Close the leaf around the rice and fold the ends together to seal.

If boiling:

1. Put the suman in a big pot so the folded side faces down. To keep the suman from moving, fill it with water and put something heavy on it, such as a plate or another piece of banana leaf. Put the lid on top and boil for 45 to 60 minutes or until the rice is fully cooked.

If steaming:

1. Put enough water in a big pot to sit below the steamer. Lay the folded side of the suman down on the steamer. Steaming will fully cook the rice in 45 to 60 minutes.
2. Take the suman off the heat. Allow it to cool a bit, then carefully peel it open. You can put coconut sugar or anything else on top of it. Enjoy!

8. MAJA BLANCA (COCONUT PUDDING WITH CORN)

Prep Time: 5 Minutes | Cook Time: 13 Minutes | Total Time: 18 Minutes | Serving: 8

Ingredients

- 80 grams corn kernel
- 300 grams sweetened condensed milk
- 380 ml evaporated milk or milk
- 40 grams desiccated coconut
- 100 grams cornstarch
- butter or margarine
- 1 can coconut milk

Instructions

1. Use butter or margarine to grease a square pan that is 21x21 cm. Put away.
2. In a pot, mix coconut milk, milk, and condensed milk. Cook over medium-low heat, turning occasionally.
3. Put the kernel of corn in. When you add the cornstarch mixture, stir it quickly and continuously until it becomes a paste-like consistency. Take it off the heat and immediately put it in a greased pan. A couple of light taps on the kitchen table should get rid of any stuck bubbles. Then, use a spatula or spoon to make the surface even. Allow the Maja Blanca to calm down and become less hot.
4. Toast the coconut flakes in a pan over low heat until they turn brown. Stir them constantly to prevent them from burning. Remove from the pan and put away.
5. Toast some coconut flakes and sprinkle them on top.

9. PICHI-PICHI (CASSAVA AND COCONUT DESSERT)

Prep Time: 15 Minutes | Cook Time: 45 Minutes | Total Time: 1 Hour | Serving: 5

Ingredients

- 1 cup of sugar
- 1/2 tsp lye water
- 1 cup of coconut
- 2 cups of water
- 1/2 tsp buko-pandan essence
- 2 cups of cassava

Instructions

1. Put potatoes, sugar, and water in a mixing bowl and mix them well.
2. While stirring the mixture all the time, add the lye water.
3. Add the buko-pandan flavor and remix it.
4. Once the batter is spread out evenly, pour it into separate cup of molds and steam them in a frying pan.
5. Steam the blend for 45 minutes to an hour or until the color turns clear.
6. Wait at least 40 minutes to an hour for the steamed pichi-pichi to cool. After at least 15 minutes, you can even put it in the fridge. Then, take it out of the molds.
7. Roll each piece in the coconut flakes.
8. Place on a serving plate, then serve. Enjoy!

10. PUTO BUMBONG (PURPLE RICE CAKE)

Prep Time: 20 Minutes | Cook Time: 15 MinutesTotal Time: 35 Minutes | Serving: 2

Ingredients

- 1 tbsp Butter or margarine
- 1 cup of glutinous rice flour
- ½ cup of coconut
- ¼ tsp violet liquid food color
- 6 tbsp water
- 3 tbsp Brown sugar or muscovado
- cheese optional

Instructions

1. Cut pieces of foil into long, thin tubes about 4 inches long and ¾ inches thick. Make eight to ten.
2. Put water and food color in a small bowl and mix them.
3. In a separate bowl, add the sticky rice flour. Mix it well with a spoon when you add colored water, two tbsp at a time.Once all the liquid is added, mix it by hand, breaking up any clumps into small grains or bits with your fingers.
4. Spread a lot of butter or margarine on the foil shape. Fill each jar with the sticky rice mix.
5. For 10 to 15 minutes, steam. Take them off the heat and let them cool down a bit.
6. Up to four or five logs should be placed on a banana leaf brushed with butter or margarine.
7. Use butter or margarine to cover the top and sides. Then, sprinkle grated coconut and brown sugar or muscovado sugar on top. You can add sliced paneer or toasted sesame seeds if you like.

11. LATIK (COCONUT RICE CAKE)

Prep Time: 5 Minutes | Cook Time: 3 Hours | Total Time: 3 Hours 5 Minutes | Serving: 20

Ingredients

- 2 cups of Un Glutinous Rice
- 2 cans Coconut Milk for Latik
- ¼ tsp Salt
- 1 cup of Brown Sugar packed
- 2 cups of Un Black Glutinous Rice

Instructions

1. Combine the coconut curds. Add the coconut milk to a pot or pan set on medium heat and boil it. Reduce the heat and cook until it becomes thick.
2. Cook the rice the way you normally would while you wait.
3. Begin scraping slowly and gently from the outside as the coconut milk gets thicker. The Coconut Curds will separate from the oil and turn from white to golden brown as you scrape the sides and bottom. Plus, stir it every so often to help it cook evenly.
4. Once the coconut curds are golden brown, save two tbsp for topping later. Then, add the Brown Sugar, Salt, and cooked Glutinous Rice. Ensure that the oil covers the rice and that the sugar is spread out evenly and has melted completely before folding cautiously.
5. While stirring and turning the rice cake every 5 to 10 minutes, keep cooking until it comes together, and all the rice is covered with the coconut oil and curd mixture.
6. The rice is done when it all comes together. Still, you can check the rice to see if it's cooked how you like it. After putting the dish in a container, spread the coconut curds on top of it.

12. BUCAYO (COCONUT AND RICE CAKE)

Prep Time: 5 Minutes | Cook Time: 20 Minutes

Total Time: 25 Minutes | Serving: 6

Ingredients

- 2 cups of coconut strings from young coconut
- 1 ½ cups of brown sugar
- ¼ cup of coconut water or just plain water

Instructions

1. Warm up a nonstick pan and add coconut water. Slowly mix the two until the coconut water turns into a thick sauce.
2. Add the coconut strings and mix them until the syrup fully covers them. Let it cook on low heat until the syrup thins out and gets even thicker.
3. When the syrup thickens, remove the pan from the heat and set it on the counter with a trivet or hot stand under it.
4. Hold off until the syrup stops fizzing and becomes a little less hot. Then, keep stirring the mixture until it melts and turns clear as it becomes thick and sticky.
5. Put some of the mixture on top of a banana leaf. Shape into a round, flat ball, and repeat with the rest of the dough.
6. Let it cool down all the way and set, then carefully take them off the banana leaves.
7. Move to a serving plate or a jar with a lid to store.

FRUIT-BASED DESSERTS

13. HALO-HALO (MIXED SHAVED ICE DESSERT)

Prep Time: 5 Minutes | Total Time: 5 Minutes | Serving: 1

Ingredients

- ¼ cup of milk or evaporated
- 1 tsp sugar if needed
- 1 tbsp leche flan topping
- 1 tsp nata de coco coconut gel
- 1 tsp sweetened saba
- 1 cup of or shaved ice
- 1 tbsp ube jam
- 1 tsp sweetened red munggo
- 1 tsp coconut strips
- 1 tsp sweetened sweet potatoes
- 1 tsp sago or tapioca pearls
- 1 tsp of sweetened langka jack fruit
- 1 tsp sweetened garbanzos

Instructions

1. Put one tsp of each item you chose into a tall glass.
2. You can add sugar if you want to. Put as much shaved ice as you can in the glass. Add more and push it down. Add milk on top. Choose the toppings you want to use.
3. Use a long spoon to mix it (a "halo"), and then enjoy it.

14. TURON (BANANA SPRING ROLLS)

Prep Time: 30 Minutes | Cook Time: 30 Minutes | Total Time: 1 Hour | Serving: 8

Ingredients

- 250 ml canola oil
- 1/8 tsp cornstarch
- 1/2 tsp ground cinnamon
- 8 pcs 8×8 inch spring roll wrapper
- 2 pcs ripe plantain
- 110 grams brown sugar

Instructions

1. Mix ½ cups of brown sugar and ½ tsp of ground cinnamon in a medium bowl.
2. When you look down at it, put a spring roll wrapper on the counter to look like a diamond.
3. Cover a cut plantain piece in the sugar and cinnamon mixture all the way through. After that, lay it flat in the middle of your diamond.
4. To wrap the plantain, do the bottom, sides, and finally, the top, like you're making a bag that will fit the plantain snugly. Roll it away from you slowly until there is a small triangle flap on top. Put a lot of the cornstarch mix on the flap and then close it.
5. Once the plantains are wrapped up, prepare your oil for frying. If you're using a deep fryer, set it to 338°F (or close to that; each one is different, like ovens). Put some paper towels on a baking sheet to prepare them while you wait for the oil to get hot enough. This is where you'll put the Turon to drain the oil after frying them. As you read on, they're done when both sides are golden brown.
6. Before you serve, let the turn cool down a bit. Adding ice cream and salted caramel sauce on top is optional but highly suggested!

15. MINATAMIS NA SAGING (SWEETENED BANANA)

Prep Time: 10 Minutes | Cook Time: 30 Minutes | Total Time: 40 Minutes | Serving: 4

Ingredients

- 3/4 cup of brown sugar
- 4 pieces saba banana saging na saba
- 1 tsp vanilla extract
- 1 1/2 cups of water
- 1/4 tsp salt

Instructions

1. Put water in a hot pot and let it boil. Stir in the brown sugar until it's mixed in. Put in the vanilla extract and salt and mix well. Set the heat to medium and add the plantains. Let it cook on low heat for 8 to 12 minutes or until the juice thickens. Turn off heat and allow the plantains to cool.

16. MANGO FLOAT (REFRIGERATED MANGO DESSERT)

Prep Time: 20 Minutes | Total Time: 20 Minutes | Serving: 9

Ingredients

- 2 cups of heavy whipping cream
- 4 Ripe mangos
- 15 Graham Crackers
- 1 tsp Vanilla extract
- ½ cup of condensed milk

Instructions

1. Wrap parchment paper around an 8x8-inch baking dish, leaving about an inch extra on each side to help you lift the cake out of the pan when ready to serve it.
2. For 30 minutes or overnight in the fridge, chill the condensed milk.
3. Peel four bananas. Get rid of the sides (fat) of the pit. Spread the mango slices out flat on a cutting board. From the four mangoes you have, cut the meat into thin slices along the length of three of them and cubes for the fourth. Save for later. On medium-high speed, whip heavy cream with an electric hand mixer or a stand mixer tool to whisk until soft to medium peaks form. Lastly, add the vanilla extract and sweetened condensed milk. Batter everything at medium to high speed until stiff, smooth peaks form.
4. Divide the whipped cream recipe into three equal parts and make a three-layer mango float. Remember to put them away. Place Graham crackers along the bottom of a rectangle or square pan. Use scissors or a sharp knife if the crackers need to be cut down.
5. Spread one-third of the cream mixture equally over the crackers. On top, put some mango pieces.
6. Do this three times so that you have three layers. To finish, add the cream, crushed graham crackers, and cubed mangos on top. Adding many layers is fine.
7. Cover, put in the fridge for 8 hours or overnight to set fully, then serve.
8. After the mango graham cake has set, take the pan out of the fridge.
9. Remove the cake from the pan carefully and place it on a cake board or work surface. Use the extra paper as a handle and lift the cake straight up. Be careful when taking the cake out of the pan.
10. Cut it into pieces of the right size and serve them cold. Enjoy!

17. BANANA CUE (CARAMELIZED BANANAS)

Prep Time: 5 Minutes | Cook Time: 15 Minutes

Total Time: 20 Minutes | Serving: 6

Ingredients

- 1 cup of brown sugar
- 12 pieces saba Banana
- 2 cups of oil

Instructions

1. Peel the bananas, then set them aside.
2. In a large pan or wok, heat the oil over medium-low heat.
3. Cook the bananas in hot oil until they turn a light brown color. Once they are done, sprinkle them with brown sugar. After mixing, add more sugar, if necessary, until all sides are covered.
4. You can remove them from the heat once the sugar has melted and turned a dark golden brown. Skewer two bananas, each using two bamboo sticks.

18. GINATAANG BILO-BILO (STICKY RICE BALLS IN COCONUT MILK)

Prep Time: 5 Minutes | Cook Time: 20 Minutes

Total Time: 25 Minutes | Serving: 5

Ingredients

- 4 saba bananas
- pinch of salt
- 1 medium cassava aka yuca
- 1 can ripe jackfruit
- 1 cup of water
- 1/4 cup of + 1 tbsp sugar
- 2 cans full fat coconut milk

Instructions

1. Make purple bilo, and swap out the pandan extract for ube extract. To make plain white bilo bilo, leave out the extract altogether.
2. Jamba, bananas, and cassava should all be cut into thin slices.
3. Sugar, salt, and water should all be mixed in a big pot. Over medium heat, bring to a simmer.
4. Add the cassava and cook until it gets soft, about 10 to 15 minutes.
5. Put in the jackfruit and saba banana. Bring it back to a boil, and then add the bilo bilo.
6. Remove from heat when everything is hot all the way through. Serve after it's cool!

19. MANGO SAGO (MANGO AND TAPIOCA DESSERT)

Prep Time: 10 Minutes | Cook Time: 10 Minutes | Total Time: 20 Minutes | Serving: 4

Ingredients

- ¼ cup of heavy cream
- ¼ cup of sweetened condensed milk
- ¾ cup of evaporated milk
- 3 ripe mangos
- ¾ cup of tapioca balls

Instructions

1. Cut the mango into even pieces, and then put half of them in a blender with heavy cream, condensed milk, and evaporated milk. Blend until smooth, and that's your base.
2. Heat water in a pot. Then, add the tapioca balls and let them cook for 10 minutes. This step is important to keep moving so they don't stick and burn. Of course, the water will start to get thicker. It's done when the tapioca is clear, and there are no more white spots.
3. Strain and rinse with cold water immediately until only tapioca remains. If you're not going to mix the tapioca into the mango sauce right away, put it in cold water so it doesn't stick together.
4. Put the creamy mango base, tapioca, and the rest of the mango chunks in a bowl and mix them. Besides the pineapple, you can now add any other fresh fruit you like.
5. Put it on a plate and top it with more mangos.

20. MANGO GRAHAM CAKE

Prep Time: 5 Minutes | Cook Time: 20 Minutes | Total Time: 25 Minutes | Serving: 8

Ingredients

- 3 cups of heavy cream
- 64 Biscoff cookies
- 6 ripe yellow mangoes
- ½ can of condensed milk

Instructions

1. Peel the bananas and cut them up. Cut two mangoes into thin slices for decorations and four into small cubes to use as layers. If you want to make the layers, you can cut them into small cubes instead of thick slices, but cutting them into cubes makes them easier to serve.
2. In a large bowl, whisk the heavy cream on medium speed until it is thick enough to form ribbons but not quite at the stiff peak stage. When you add the sweetened condensed milk to the whipped cream, keep whisking it on medium speed until it forms stiff peaks. Be careful not to mix too much. Get a 9x9 baking pan ready. Line the float with parchment paper, leaving extra hanging on both sides to make lifting out of the pan easy when it's time to serve. If not, you can serve it straight from the pan without lining it. To start, put a layer of Biscoff cookies at the bottom of the pan. Cover the cookies with a third of the whipped cream mixture. Cover the top with a thick layer of chopped or sliced mangoes. Add more cookies, whipped cream, and fruits for the second layer, and repeat the steps above. Add the last few cookies and the rest of the whipped cream to the third and final layer. Put thinly sliced mangoes on top and then crush Biscoff cookies to finish. Put the pan in the fridge overnight to set. Cover it with cling wrap.
3. Cut the mango float into pieces the next day, and enjoy!

21. FRUIT SALAD WITH CREAM AND CONDENSED MILK

Prep Time: 15 Minutes | Total Time: 15 Minutes | Serving: 6

Ingredients

- 1 tbsp golden raisins
- 2 tbsp sliced almonds
- ¼ cup of blueberries
- 1 orange pulp peel
- ½ cup of red and green grapes
- 1 apple
- 1 banana
- ½ cup of sweetened condensed milk
- ¼ tsp cardamom powder
- 5 strawberries
- ½ cup of heavy whipping cream
- Few cherries optional for garnishing

Instructions

1. Wash and dry all fruits. Peel (if required) and chop all fruits into bite-size and almost equal pieces. Add cold, heavy whipping cream to a large mixing bowl. Whip the cream until it is light and fluffy. Add the cardamom powder and condensed milk and mix well.
2. Toss in the chopped fruits, raisins, and nuts that have been sliced.
3. Cover, and put in the fridge for at least two hours before serving!!
4. Serve cold with extra fruits, nuts, and a cherry on top! Enjoy!

22. BUKO PANDAN (YOUNG COCONUT WITH PANDAN JELLY)

Prep Time: 30 Minutes | Cook Time: 10 Minutes | Total Time: 40 Minutes | Serving: 12

Ingredients

- ½ cup of tapioca pearls
- 1 bottle coconut gel
- 3 cups of coconut juice
- 1 can sweetened condensed milk
- 2 cups of coconut meat
- 1 pack all-purpose cream
- 1 bottle kaong
- ½ cup of sugar
- ½ pouch jelly powder
- 6-8 pieces Pandan leaves

Instructions

1. Put the gulaman or jelly powder in a pot and add the coconut juice. Stir to mix. After adding the sugar and pandan leaves, boil them while stirring constantly.
2. Once it starts to boil, remove it from the heat and pour it into a square pan to cool and set. For faster results, put it in the fridge. Remove the gelatin from the heat and cut it into cubes.
3. Cook the tapioca pearls while you wait. Heat 1 liter of water in a pot. Toss in the tiny pieces of sago or tapioca. Cook for 15 minutes or until they become clear. Stir them every so often so they don't stick together. Remove from heat and strain the sago pearls using a fine sieve. Rinse the sago or tapioca pieces well until they are no longer hot to the touch. Save for later.
4. Cream and sweetened condensed milk should be mixed in a large bowl. Add the pandan jelly cubes, kaong, nata de coco, and coconut strips, and mix them gently until well combined.
5. Cover the bowl and put it in the fridge to cool down. If you want to freeze it, move the food to another container.

23. CASSAVA CAKE

Prep Time: 15 Minutes | Cook Time: 1 Hour | Total Time: 1 Hour 15 Minutes | Serving: 6

Ingredients

- 1/4 cup of butter
- 2 cups of coconut milk
- 14 tbsp granulated white sugar
- 2 packs cassava
- 6 tbsp cheddar cheese
- 1/2 cup of condensed milk
- 3 pieces egg
- 1/2 12 ounce . can evaporated milk

Topping:

- 2 tbsp cheddar cheese
- 2 cups of coconut milk
- 2 tbsp sugar
- 1/2 cup of condensed milk
- 2 tbsp flour

Instructions

1. Add the chopped cassava, butter, 1/2 cup condensed milk, 1/2 cup evaporated milk, six tbsp cheddar cheese, 14 tbsp sugar, and two eggs in a mixing bowl. Mix the ingredients well.
2. Put the two cups of coconut milk in the bowl with the other ingredients, which have already been mixed, and mix it again. First, grease the baking sheet. Then, pour in the batter made of the things you just mixed. Put the baking sheet with the batter in it and heat the oven to 350 degrees Fahrenheit for 10 minutes. Then, take it out and bake it for an hour. Take it out of the oven and set it away. While that is going on, make the topping by mixing two tbsp of sugar and flour in a hot pot. Add half a cup of condensed milk and mix well. While stirring all the time, add two tbsp of cheddar cheese. Add 2 cups of coconut milk and stir it for 10 minutes. Cover the baked Cassava Cake with the filling and spread it out evenly. Take the last egg and separate the yolk from the egg white. We only need the egg white. Use a basting brush to cover the topping with the egg white glaze. To make the cassava cake, dip the brush in the egg white and brush it on.
3. Turn on the heat setting in your oven. Place the cassava cake under the broiler until it turns a light brown. Add more chopped cheese on top to serve.

24. AVOCADO ICE CANDY

Prep Time: 10 Minutes |: Total Time: 10 Minutes | Serving: 12

Ingredients

- lemon or lime juice
- 1 can sweetened condensed milk
- 2 large avocados
- 2 cups of milk

Instructions

1. Cut the avocado in half, discard the pit, and scoop out the flesh. Add lemon or lime juice on top.
2. Put avocado, fresh milk, and condensed milk in a blender and blend until smooth.
3. Using a spoon, pour the mixed ingredients into plastic bags until they are ¾ whole, leaving about 3 inches of space around the edges. Make a knot in the last three inches of the tube so it is hard but not too tight.
4. Fill a flat container with the tubes and place them in a single layer on top of it. Freeze for 2 to 3 hours or until the tubes are solid.

CUSTARDS & PUDDINGS

25. LECHE FLAN (CARAMEL CUSTARD)

Prep Time: 10 Minutes | Cook Time: 44 Minutes | Total Time: 55 Minutes | Serving: 6

Ingredients

- 1 can condensed milk
- 1 cup of granulated sugar
- 1 tsp vanilla extract
- 1 cup of milk or evaporated milk
- 10 pieces eggs

Instructions

1. Take all the eggs and separate the egg white from the egg yolk.
2. Put the egg yolks in a large bowl and use an egg beater or a fork to beat them.
3. Mix well after adding the condensed milk.
4. Put the vanilla and fresh milk in the bowl. Mix wellPlace the mold (llanera) on the stove and heat it with a low flame.Spread the sugar crystals on the mold and mix them well until the hard sugar turns into a light brown liquid (caramel When I make leche flan, it's easier for me to use separate round pans.On the flat side of the mold, spread the caramel (liquid sugar) out evenly.
5. Wait five minutes, and then pour the egg yolk and milk mix into the mold.
6. Use aluminum foil to cover the top of the mold.
7. For 30 to 35 minutes, steam the mold with the egg and milk mix.
8. Let it cool down after steaming, then put it in the fridge.
9. Serve for dessert.

26. UBE HALAYA (PURPLE YAM PUDDING)

Prep Time: 5 Minutes | Cook Time: 35 Minutes | Total Time: 40 Minutes | Serving: 6

Ingredients

- 16 ounce ube purple yam
- coconut oil
- 1 cup of granulated sugar
- 14 ounce coconut milk
- 2 ounce water

Instructions

1. Stir the ube, coconut milk, water, and sugar in a saucepan. Set the pan over medium-low heat and boil the mixture. Turn down the heat and use an immersion blender to smooth the ube.
2. To make it thick, stir it constantly and scrape the sides of the pan. This should take about 40 minutes. You can choose the consistency you want for the halaya. The longer you cook it, the thicker it will get. Take it off the heat.
3. If you like your ube halaya shiny, add about a tsp of coconut oil and mix it in.
4. When the halaya is done, you can put it in a jar or shape it into a cake. To shape the ube halaya, use coconut oil to grease your molds or dish. Put the mixture into the molds, smooth the tops, and cover them with plastic wrap. Refrigerate for at least an hour to cool completely. It can be served right away or refrigerated overnight.

27. YEMA (CUSTARD CANDY)

Prep Time: 20 Minutes | Cook Time: 20 Minutes | Total Time: 40 Minutes | Serving: 28

Ingredients

- 3 egg yolks
- 2 tbsp butter
- ¼ cup of nuts
- ¼ cup of granulated sugar
- 1 can condensed milk

Instructions

1. Using low heat, melt the butter in a medium-sized pot.
2. Beat in the sweet milk and mix it in. Filipino custard.
3. Carefully stir in the eggs. Stir the mixture for five more minutes or until it becomes thicker. This is Filipino custard.
4. Add the nuts and mix them well.
5. Add more cooking time until the mixture is stretchy. Remove it from the heat and let it cool until it's comfortable to roll into balls.
6. When it's cool enough to touch, put a tbsp of the mixture in your clean hands and roll it into a ball.
7. After dipping, set it away.
8. You can immediately serve the candies in a serving dish with colorful picks or wrap each in cellophane or wax paper to make it look nice.

28. CREMA DE FRUTA (LAYERED CAKE WITH CUSTARD)

Prep Time: 20 Minutes | Cook Time: 35 Minutes

Total Time: 55 Minutes | Serving: 8

Ingredients

- 1 3/4 cups of sugar
- 1 tsp baking powder
- 4 cups of milk
- 2 tbsp unflavored gelatin
- 8 pieces egg yolks
- 1/3 cup of butter
- 2 1/4 cups of water
- 1 1/2 cup of flour
- 1 big can fruit cocktail
- 1 1/2 tsp vanilla extract

Instructions

1. Mix the baking powder and 1 cup of flour for the sponge cake using a flour sifter. Put away
2. In a mixing bowl, add four egg whites and beat them until the mixture gets thick.
3. Slowly add 1/2 cup of sugar while beating the egg.
4. As you go, slowly add the sifted flour and baking powder mix. Thoroughly mix the items.
5. Mix 1 cup of milk, butter, and vanilla extract in a saucepan. Then, cook until the butter melts.
6. Add the cooked mixture to the bowl and mix it with the rest of the ingredients until they are evenly distributed.
7. Warm the oven up to 350°F.
8. Mix the ingredients and pour them into a baking pan. Bake for 23 minutes or until the sponge cake is done. Put away.
9. Warm up a pot and add 1/4 cup of sugar to it. This will make the simple syrup.
10. Add 1/4 cup of water immediately and cook until the sugar is gone. Then, let it cool for a few minutes.
11. Put the simple syrup on the sponge cake and then spread it out.
12. Mix 1/2 cup of flour, 1 cup of sugar, and 3 cups of milk in a pot to make the custard. Cook while stirring the mixture until it becomes thick.
13. Add half of the cooked mixture to the bowl with the egg yolks and mix it well.
14. Add the rest of the items to the saucepan with everything else. This is now the custard. Mix until the thickness is thick enough.
15. Spread the custard layer out evenly on top of the sponge cake.
16. Take the fruit cocktail out of the liquid concentrate and set it away.
17. Lay out all of the fruits on top of the custard. Arrange them in a sensible way.
18. Mix two cups of water with the gelatin.
19. Melt the gelatin and fruit cocktail concentrate in a pot. Then add hot water and bring to a boil.
20. When it starts to boil, remove it from the heat and let it cool until slightly warmer than room temperature.
21. Place the gelatin mixture on top of the fruit cocktail layer and refrigerate for at least one hour.
22. Serve chilled for dessert.

29. DULCE DE LECHE

Prep Time: 10 Minutes | Cook Time: 3 Hours

Total Time: 3 Hours 10 Minutes | Serving: 4

Ingredients

- 14 ounce sweetened condensed milk

Instructions

1. Warm the oven to 425°F. Put the sweetened condensed milk in a pie plate or cake pan and cover it tightly with foil. Put the meat in a deep cooking pan and add enough hot water to cover it by about an inch.
2. Put it in the oven for 12 and a half hours. You can add or subtract bake time depending on how dark you want the color. Let it cool down, then use a whisk to remove any lumps and smooth the mixture.

30. TAHO (SILKEN TOFU WITH SYRUP AND TAPIOCA)

Prep Time: 5 Minutes | Cook Time: 15 Minutes

Total Time: 20 Minutes | Serving: 4

Ingredients

- 1 1/4 cups of brown sugar
- 1 cup of water
- 16 ounce silken tofu
- 1 cup of tapioca or sago pearls
- 1 tsp vanilla

Instructions

1. Warm up a big pot of water. Follow the directions on the package to cook the tapioca pearls. You can do this before you start. Store the pearls with water or brown sugar syrup.
2. Put the vanilla, water, and brown sugar in a small pot and set it over medium-high heat. Bring to a boil, then boil the heat to a simmer and stir to break up the sugar. Simmer for another two to four minutes, then take it off the heat. You can also make this sauce, called arnibal, ahead of time.
3. Put the soft tofu in a steamer lined with parchment paper. Steam for 10 to 15 minutes or until everything is hot. You can heat the tofu in the microwave for two to five minutes.
4. To serve, put warm, soft tofu slices into a small cup of . Add tapioca or sago pearls and pour a caramelized brown sugar syrup over them. Serve right away while still warm.

31. MAJA MAIS (CORN PUDDING)

Prep Time: 5 Minutes | Cook Time: 13 Minutes

Total Time: 18 Minutes | Serving: 10

Ingredients

- 1 ½ cup of evaporated milk
- butter or margarine
- ½ cup of corn kernel
- ½ cup of desiccated coconut
- 1 cup of sweetened condensed milk
- ¾ cup of cornstarch
- 1 can coconut milk

Instructions

1. Use butter or margarine to grease a square pan that is 21x21 cm. Put away.
2. In a pot, mix coconut milk, milk, and condensed milk. Cook over medium-low heat, turning now and then.
3. Put the kernel of corn in. When you add the cornstarch mixture, stir it quickly and continuously until it becomes a paste-like consistency. Take it off the heat and immediately put it in a greased pan. A couple of light taps on the kitchen table should get rid of any stuck bubbles. Then, use a spatula or spoon to make the surface even. Allow the Maja Blanca to calm down and become less hot.
4. Toast the coconut flakes in a pan over low heat until they turn brown. Stir them constantly to prevent them from burning. Remove from the pan and put away.
5. Toast some coconut flakes and sprinkle them on top.

32. EGG PIE

Prep Time: 10 Minutes | Cook Time: 40 Minutes | Total Time: 50 Minutes | Serving: 6

Ingredients

Pie Crust:

- 2 tbsp granulated sugar
- 2 1/2 cups of all-purpose flour
- 1 tsp salt
- 1/4 to 1/2 cup of cold water
- 1 cup of unsalted butter

Filling:

- 1 3/4 cups of evaporated milk
- 1 cup of granulated sugar
- 1 piece egg white
- 3 pieces raw eggs
- 1 tsp vanilla extract

Instructions

1. Put the flour, sugar, and salt together and mix them well to make the crust.
2. In the middle, add the butter and use a pastry machine to mix it in.
3. Pour the cold water in slowly while mixing the ingredients. Keep mixing until all of the ingredients are well mixed in.
4. Gather the dough and make it into a ball.
5. Put the dough in the fridge for at least 30 minutes to make the butter hard.
6. Put flour on a clean surface and use a rolling pin to flatten the dough in the fridge. Smoothing the dough should be big enough to fit over a 9-inch round baking pan.
7. Spread the flattened dough on top of the baking pan. Cut off the extra edge with scissors.
8. Put it in the fridge while you fill it.
9. Warm the evaporated milk in the microwave for two minutes to start making the filling.
10. Put the three raw eggs and the egg yolk into a large bowl.
11. While whisking, add the white sugar little by little.
12. Add the vanilla extract and whisk until all the ingredients are well mixed.
13. Pour in the hot milk and mix it in well.
14. With an electric mixer, beat the egg white, which has been separated, until it makes soft peaks.
15. Mix the egg white made into the milk, eggs, and sugar.
16. Warm the oven up to 350°F.
17. Put the filling mixture on top of the pie shell that has been chilled.
18. Bake at 350°F for 15 minutes. Then, lower the heat to 325°F and bake for another 30 to 40 minutes.
19. Take the egg pie out of the oven and let it cool down.
20. Serve for dessert.

33. PASTILLAS DE LECHE (MILK CANDIES)

Prep Time: 15 Minutes | Cook Time: 1 Hour 30 Minutes

Total Time: 1 Hour 45 Minutes | Serving: 4

Ingredients

- 2 ounces powdered whole milk
- 2 ounces granulated sugar
- 2 cups of milk
- 3 fluid ounces heavy cream
- 1/8 tsp kosher salt

Instructions

1. Mix milk and heavy cream in a 10-inch stainless steel skillet. Heat over medium-low heat and bring to a simmer. Use a rubber spatula to stir the mixture every so often so that skin doesn't form on the pan's walls. Lower the heat to a low level and keep turning and scraping the pan often for about 30 minutes or until the mixture is reduced by half.
2. Add the salt and sugar and mix well. Continue cooking and turning often until the mixture thickens into a paste-like substance. You'll know it's done when you drag a spatula along the bottom of the pan, and the milk mixture slowly fills the space. This should take about an hour.
3. Move the milk paste to a medium-sized heatproof bowl. You should have about 3/4 cup of it. Add the powdered milk and stir until everything is well-mixed. For about 30 seconds, keep stirring until no more dry powder and a sticky dough forms. Wait about 30 minutes for it to cool down to room temperature. Put the bowl in the fridge for at least one hour and up to eight hours or until it is cold. Cover it with plastic wrap.
4. Spray cooking spray on your hands and move the chilled dough to a clean cutting board. Roll the dough into a disk about 5 inches long with your hands. Cut the cylinder half across the middle with a cutting knife or a bench scraper. Make a 5-inch-long disk out of each piece. Cut each disk into eight equal pieces. With your hands, roll each piece into a 2-inch-long cylinder between your fingers. Pastillas can now be put in a jar that won't let air in and kept in the fridge for up to a week until they are ready to be served.
5. Put 1/2 cup of sugar in a wide, flat bowl before you are ready to serve. Put up to four pastillas in the bowl at a time and shake it to cover the pieces with sugar on all sides. Place the pastillas that have been covered in sugar on a serving plate. Repeat the coating process with the rest of the pastillas. Serve.

34. PUTO FLAN

Prep Time: 10 Minutes | Cook Time: 15 Minutes | Total Time: 25 Minutes | Serving: 12

Ingredients

- butter - , for greasing the molds

Egg Custard:

- 4 egg yolks
- ¾ cup of sweetened condensed milk
- 1 tbsp vanilla extract

Puto Batter:

- 2 egg whites
- ½ cup of fresh milk
- 1 cup of all-purpose flour
- ½ cup of sugar
- ½ tbsp baking powder

Instructions

1. Melt some butter and use it to brush the shapes. Whisk the egg whites, sweetened condensed milk, and vanilla extract until well mixed. Fill each dish a third of the way with the custard mix. Let it steam for 5 minutes. Make the Puto batter at the same time. First, use an electric mixer to beat the egg whites until a soft peak forms. Add the fresh milk and keep beating. After you add the flour, sugar, and baking powder, beat for one or two more minutes. Fill about ¾ of the shapes with Puto batter and pour it on the steamed custard. Steam for another 10 to 12 minutes or until a stick inserted comes out clean. Take them out of the molds after they have cooled down a bit.

35. COCONUT CUSTARD (MAJA BLANCA)

Prep Time: 5 Minutes | Cook Time: 15 Minutes | Total Time: 20 Minutes | Serving: 10

Ingredients

- ½ cup of desiccated coconut
- ½ cup of corn kernel
- 1 ½ cup of evaporated milk
- ¾ cup of cornstarch
- butter or margarine
- 1 cup of sweetened condensed milk
- 1 can coconut milk

Instructions

1. Use butter or margarine to grease a square pan that is 21x21 cm. Put away. In a pot, mix coconut milk, milk, and condensed milk. Cook over medium-low heat, turning occasionally.
2. Put the kernel of corn in. When you add the cornstarch mixture, stir it quickly and continuously until it becomes a paste-like consistency. Take it off the heat and immediately put it in a greased pan. A couple of light taps on the kitchen table should get rid of any stuck bubbles. Then, use a spatula or spoon to make the surface even. Allow the Maja Blanca to calm down and become less hot. Toast the coconut flakes in a pan over low heat until they turn brown. Stir them constantly to prevent them from burning. Remove from the pan and put away.
3. Toast some coconut flakes and sprinkle them on top.

36. SAPIN-SAPIN CUSTARD

Prep Time: 10 Minutes | Cook Time: 50 Minutes

Total Time: 1 Hour | Serving: 12

Ingredients

- 1 cup of coconut cream
- 2 cans coconut milk
- 1 cup of sugar
- 1 can condensed milk
- 3 drops langka flavor extract
- 3 ½ cups of glutinous rice flour
- 3 drops ube flavor extract

Instructions

1. Put the coconut cream in a pan and set it on medium heat. Cook, stirring occasionally, until the liquid begins to thicken.
2. Turn down the heat and keep cooking. As the oil separates and lumps form, stir and scrape the pan's sides and bottom often to prevent burning. Stir and cook some more until the curds turn golden brown.
3. Latik should be kept in different containers until it is time to use. Let the oil drain off of it.
4. Brush the oil all over the inside of the bottom and inside sides of an 8-inch round baking pan.
5. Glutinous rice flour, coconut milk, condensed milk, and sugar should all be mixed in a big bowl. Mix and stir until the sugar is gone, smooth, and well-mixed.
6. Use a fine-mesh sieve to separate the batter into three bowls of the same size.
7. To spread the color, put the ube extract in one bowl and stir it around. Then, add the langka extract to a different bowl and mix the color well. The rest of the area will be plain white.
8. Pour the ube-flavored batter into the baking pan. Steam it for about 10 minutes, or until it's set and a toothpick stuck in it comes out clean.
9. Carefully pour the batter that tastes like langka over the purple layer. Steam it for about 10 minutes, or until it's set and a toothpick stuck in it comes out clean.
10. Pour plain batter slowly over the yellow layer. Steam it for about 10 minutes, or until it's set and a toothpick stuck in it comes out clean.
11. Take the cake pan out of the steamer and let it cool down.
12. Run a knife around the sides to remove the rice cake from the pan. Lay a large, flat serving plate on top of the cake pan and carefully flip it over. A few taps on the pan will slide the sapin-sapin onto the dish. The purple layer will now be on top.
1. Brush a lot of coconut oil on the top and sides of the sapin sapin. Put latik on top of the cake and cut it into serving sizes.

ICE CREAM & FROZEN DESSERTS

37. UBE ICE CREAM

Prep Time: 20 Minutes | Cook Time: 40 Minutes

Total Time: 1 Hour | Serving: 6

Ingredients

- 5 egg yolks
- 1 cup of heavy cream
- ¼ cup of ube halaya
- ½ cup of granulated sugar
- 1 cup of whole milk
- 1 tsp vanilla extract
- 1 tsp ube extract

Instructions

1. Put the heavy cream and whole milk in a saucepan and heat until smoke comes from them. Then, take the heat off.
2. Put the sugar and egg whites in a small bowl and mix them. Whisk for about 30 seconds or until the mixture turns a smooth, yellow color.
3. Mix the eggs with 1/4 cup of the hot cream and whisk them until smooth and uniformly yellow. In this step, raise the temperature of the eggs so they don't cook through the hot cream. Add the eggs and hot milk to the pan.
4. Add ube and vanilla flavor.
5. Bring the heat back on. Stir it and heat it up to 170 degrees F. To see if it's done, put some cream on the back of a spoon and run your finger through it. When the cream is done, it should have a thick, smooth line that doesn't break. Take the cream off the heat.
6. Using a fine mesh sieve, pour the cream into a big bowl. This will remove any milk or egg lumps.
7. Put in the ube halaya. Mix it into the cream using an electric blender. You can also use a standard blender for this step.
8. Bring the cream to room temperature, then cool it in the fridge for 6 to 8 hours, which makes the texture creamier.
9. Start an ice cream maker and put the cream in it. Churn it for 10 to 15 minutes. The ice cream you make should be harder than soft serve.
10. Put the ice cream in a jar in the freezer and freeze it overnight.

38. BUKO SALAD ICE CREAM

Prep Time: 4 Hours 15 Minutes | Total Time: 4 Hours 15 Minutes | Serving: 6

Ingredients

For the ice cream:

- 1 cup of all purpose cream
- 1 can sweetened condensed milk
- 8-10 pandan leaves
- 3/4 cup of thick coconut milk/cream
- Green buko pandan food colouring/flavouring (optional)

To serve with (optional):

- Buko pandan jelly
- Lychees
- Cornflakes
- Shredded coconut meat

Instructions

1. Put the all-purpose cream, coconut milk, and pandan leaves in a food processor or heavy-duty blender. Blitz or blend for a few minutes until the pandan leaves are chopped very small.
2. Pour the cream and coconut milk mixed with pandan over a fine sieve into a big, chilled mixing bowl. Press down hard on the pandan leaf pulp with the back of a spoon to extract all the liquid. Strain the cream mixture through the strainer. Throw away the pandan leaf pulp.
3. Wash the cream mixed with pandan with an electric hand-held mixer until soft peaks form. Add the sweetened milk. At this point, you could also add a little vanilla extract. Whip it some more until it forms soft peaks. It should be fluffy and mousse-like.
4. Put it in a jar that won't let air in and freeze for 4 or 24 hours. Every 30 minutes, check on the mixture and use a spoon to mix it (churn) so that it doesn't turn into granita, which is coarse flavored ice.
5. It should be left at room temperature for about 15 minutes before being scooped out and served. For an extra crunch, it can be served plain or with fresh coconut meat, buko pandan jelly, other fruits, or crushed cornflakes. Enjoy!

39. AVOCADO ICE CREAM

Prep Time: 5 Minutes | Cook Time: 1 Hour 5 Minutes

Total Time: 1 Hour 10 Minutes | Serving: 4

Ingredients

- 3/4 cup of sugar
- 1 cup of mint
- 1 cup of heavy cream
- 1 1/2 cups of coconut milk
- 2 large avocados

Instructions

1. Put everything into a high-speed blender and blend it until it's smooth.
2. Put the mixture into a bowl and chill it in the fridge for three hours to make it thicker.
3. Put the chilled avocado ice cream mix into an ice cream maker and churn it. You can also put it in a jar and freeze it that way. Make sure to mix it every 30 minutes so it doesn't freeze.
4. Before you serve, let the ice cream sit at room temperature for 15 minutes.

40. MANGO ICE CREAM

Prep Time: 15 Minutes | Cook Time: 6 Hours

Total Time: 6 Hours 15 Minutes | Serving: 8

Ingredients

- 1 can sweetened condensed milk
- 2 cups of heavy cream
- 2 large mangoes
- 2 drops yellow food coloring, optional

Instructions

1. Slice mangoes and scoop flesh, discarding pit and skin. Process mangoes in a blender or food processor to an applesauce-like consistency.
2. Mix mango pulp, condensed milk, and heavy cream in a big bowl.
3. Beat the mixture with an electric mixer set to low speed until it becomes thicker. Slow down to medium speed and keep beating for 8 to 10 minutes or until hard peaks form.
4. Add food coloring a few drops while beating until the right color is reached.
5. Put the mix into a 9-by-5-inch loaf pan. Cover with plastic film and lightly press the film against the cream mixture's surface.
6. Put it in the freezer for at least six hours or overnight. Serve frozen.

41. KESO ICE CREAM (CHEESE ICE CREAM)

Prep Time: 20 Minutes | Total Time: 20 Minutes | Serving: 24

Ingredients
- 1 can condensed milk
- 1 block processed cheese
- 1 block cream cheese
- 2 cups of all-purpose cream
- Yellow food color -optional

Instructions
1. Use a coarse cheese grater to shred the cheese. It needs to be chunky or cut up into little bits.
2. Whip cream until it's smooth, fluffy, and almost twice as big as before. Put it in the fridge until you're ready to use it.
3. Cream cheese and condensed milk should be mixed in a big bowl. Beat with a high-speed electric mixer until smooth, light, and fluffy.
4. Using a spoon, slowly fold the whipped cream into the cream cheese mixture until everything is well mixed.
5. Add the sliced cheese and a few drops of yellow food color.
6. Put the mixture in a rectangular pan or an ice cream tub. The pan may contain air bubbles. Tap it on the counter to remove them. Press a plastic wrap on the pan flat on the dish. Put it in the freezer for six hours or overnight.
7. Scoop the cheese ice cream into serving bowls or ice cream cones.

42. HALO-HALO ICE CREAM

Prep Time: 10 Minutes | Cook Time: 2 Hours | Total Time: 2 Hours 10 Minutes | Serving: 5

Ingredients
- 1/4 cup of green nata de coco
- 1/4 cup of Red beans
- 1/4 cup of Alaska Classic Evaporated Filled Milk
- 1/4 cup of Ube jam
- 1/4 cup of red kaong
- 1/4 cup of Langka
- 1/4 cup of Minatamis na saging
- 2 packs Alaska Créma
- 1 can Sweetened Condensed Filled Milk

Instructions
1. Use an electric mixer to whip chilled Alaska Créma. Once it gets thick, gradually mix while adding Alaska Condensed Filled Milk and Alaska Evaporada. After combining everything, freeze it for an hour.
2. Once the mixture is thicker and has frozen, remove the ice cream from the freezer and carefully fold the rest of the ingredients, except for the tube. Mix everything, then take a scoop of the ube and spread it in different tub parts. Put it in the freezer until you're ready to serve.
3. Add toasted pinipig and slices of leche flan on top. Use cups of to make halo-halo popsicles instead.

43. CHOCOLATE ICE CANDY

Prep Time: 5 Minutes | Cook Time: 20 Minutes

Total Time: 25 Minutes | Serving: 15

Ingredients

- 1 cup of cassava flour
- 1 can condensed milk
- brown sugar
- 1 cup of unsweetened cocoa powder
- 2 liters water
- 1 can evaporated milk
- pinipig (optional)

Instructions

1. Boil 2 liters of water.
2. Mix 1 cup of hot water with cocoa powder. Put away.
3. Add the evaporated milk, condensed milk, and cocoa powder when the water starts to boil. Check the sweetness. If necessary, add sugar. Add everything together and let it boil.
4. Break up 1 cup of room-temperature water with cassava flour. Add to the ice candy mix that is cooking. Continue to stir. Make sure there are no lumps. Let it cook for 5 minutes. After that, take it off the heat and let it cool down.
5. Put in ice candy molds after it has cooled down.

44. MANGO ICE CANDY

Prep Time: 10 Minutes | Cook Time: 10 Minutes

Total Time: 20 Minutes | Serving: 5

Ingredients

- ½ cup of granulated sugar
- 2 cups of water
- ¼ cup of cornstarch
- 12 ounce evaporated milk
- 14 ounce condensed milk
- 4 champagne mangoes

Instructions

1. Set the heat to medium-low and add the water to the big saucepan. It should now be boiling.
2. Put the mango chunks and drained milk in a blender. Mix until completely smooth.
3. Stir the cornstarch into the hot water if you're using it, then add the sugar and condensed milk. Gradually add the blended fruit mixture. Lower the heat to low and let it boil for 5 minutes, stirring until everything is well coupled. Leave the pot off the heat for about an hour to cool down.
4. Pour the mango mixture into the plastic bags until they are about three-quarters full. Seal the bags by tying a knot at the top.
5. Leave the bags in the freezer all night. Put it in the freezer until you're ready to serve.
6. Enjoy!

45. BUKO LYCHEE SORBET

Prep Time: 4 Hours 10 Minutes | Total Time: 4 Hours 10 Minutes | Serving: 6

Ingredients

- 2 cups of coconut juice
- 2 cups of young coconut
- 1 can ychee in light syrup
- ⅔ cup of sugar

Instructions

1. Add sugar, lychee (with its syrup), chopped coconut, and coconut juice to a bowl. Stir until the sugar is dissolved.
2. When solid, put it in a container with a lid that fits tightly on top and freezes for a few hours. Serve frozen.

46. MAIS CON YELO (CORN WITH SHAVED ICE)

Prep Time: 10 Minutes | Total Time: 10 Minutes | Serving: 2

Ingredients

- White Sugar
- Shaved Ice
- Evaporated Milk
- Sweetened Condensed Milk
- Sweet Corn
- Corn Flakes (Optional)
- Saging na Saba (Optional)
- Keso (Optional)

Instructions

1. Put the shaved ice on top of the sweet corn in a glass.
2. Add milk, sugar, condensed milk, and evaporated milk (adjust to taste), and mix everything with a spoon.
3. You can add things like Keso, Saging na Saba, or CornFlakes.
4. Serve immediately.

47. LANGKA ICE CREAM (JACKFRUIT ICE CREAM)

Prep Time: 2 Hours | Cook Time: 30 Minutes

Total Time: 2 Hours 34 Minutes | Serving: 8

Ingredients

- ½ cup of sugar
- 1 cup of coconut milk
- 1 cup of Jackfruit
- 1 cup of Heavy cream

Instructions

1. Set a medium-sized sauce pot on low heat and add ¼ cup of sugar. Cook the jackfruit for 30 minutes.
2. When it's cool enough to touch, blend cooked jackfruit into a smooth paste. Put it in the fridge to cool down while you make the rest of the mixture.
3. Put the heavy cream, coconut milk, and the rest of the sugar in a bowl. Mix the ingredients well. Then, add the jackfruit puree and chill the whole thing for at least two hours or overnight.
4. Make ice cream the next morning.

48. FILIPINO TAHO

Prep Time: 15 Minutes | Cook Time: 30 Minutes

Total Time: 45 Minutes | Serving: 4

Ingredients

- ½ cup of sago or tapioca pearls
- 1 18- ounce pack soft
- ¾ cup of water
- 1 cup of brown sugar
- 1 tsp vanilla extract optional

Instructions

1. Put the tofu in a boiler or steam basket and steam it for 10 to 15 minutes or until it's completely cooked.
2. In addition to making the tofu, you can work on the sago. This would depend on the type of sago you have. Some take almost an hour to cook, while others only take five minutes. When your sago is done, put it in a bowl of cold water and set it aside until you're ready to put it together.
3. Brown sugar and water should be put in a pot and slowly boiled until the sugar is completely dissolved.
4. Take it off the heat and, if you want to, add 1 tsp of vanilla extract. Stir to mix. Leave it out until you're ready to put it together.
5. Mix soy, sago, and sugar in a mug, glass, or bowl to make taho. You decide how much of each you put in.

CAKES &PASTRIES

49. BRAZO DE MERCEDES (CUSTARD ROLL)

Prep Time: 2 Hours 10 Minutes | Cook Time: 20 Minutes

Total Time: 2 Hours 30 Minutes | Serving: 12

Ingredients

Custard Filling:

- 10 egg yolks
- 1 tsp vanilla extract
- 1 CAN 14 ounce condensed milk
- 3 tbsp butter

Meringue:

- 10 egg whites
- 1 cup of sugar
- 1 tsp cream of tartar

Instructions

1. Put the 10x12-inch pan together by thoroughly greasing all sides with oil. Then, put wax paper over the pan and grease the wax paper. Using a brush or a spray can handle the oil. Set aside.
2. Combine egg whites and condensed milk in a medium-sized saucepan. Set the heat to low and cook the mixture, scraping it from side to side. Continue to stir while cooking, and add one tbsp of butter until the mixture becomes sticky.
3. Cool the filling down after taking it off the heat.

50. UBE CAKE

Prep Time: 30 Minutes | Cook Time: 1 Hour 30 Minutes

Total Time: 2 Hours | Serving: 8

Ingredients

Pan Release Grease:

- 2 tbsp flour
- 2 tbsp oil
- 2 tbsp lard or shortening

Cake Batter:

- 2 tsp vanilla extract
- 4 medium eggs at room temperature
- ½ tsp salt
- ½ cup of vegetable or coconut oil
- 1 cup of milk
- 2 tsp Ube extract
- 3 cups of all-purpose flour
- 1 cup of sugar
- ¾ to 1 cup of ube halaya or jam
- 3 tsp baking powder
- ½ cup of butter softened

Frosting:

- 1 pack 200g cream cheese
- ½ cup powdered sugar
- 2 cups whipping/heavy cream
- 1 tsp vanilla extract
- Drops of ube extract/color

Instructions

1. Put the ingredients in a small bowl and use a whisk or fork to mix them until the mixture is smooth. This will make the pan release grease. Grease the bottom and sides of a round cake pan at least 8 inches (20 cm) in diameter and 3 inches high, or use two pans.
2. Warm up your oven to 300°F (normal settings or no fan).
3. Cream the butter, oil, and sugar in a bowl using an electric mixer until light and fluffy, about two to three minutes.
4. Add the eggs one at a time and mix them until well combined. Then, mix in the ube food color or extract and vanilla extract.
5. Add the salt, baking powder, and flour all at once. (Don't mix yet). On top of the dry ingredients, add the milk and beat at medium to low speed just until everything is mixed. Do not mix too much.
6. Divide about ½ cup of the batter between two muffin tins lined with cupcake papers. You can also use a small mold or baking dish. Beat the ube jam into the rest of the batter.
7. Spread the rest of the batter evenly in the prepared pan. If you are using two pans, split the batter in half. If there is any air inside, tap the sides and bottom to remove it.
8. If you put a toothpick in the middle and it comes out clean, it's done. Bake for 50 minutes to an hour in a hot oven. If you use two pans, it might be done in 20 to 30 minutes. The cupcakes will be done in 20 to 25 minutes. It's possible to bake them both at the same time. After 20 to 25 minutes, turn the cupcakes out.

9. Take a break and let the cupcakes cool down. Remove the bags and use your hands to break them up into chunks or crumbs. Then, spread the mixture on a baking sheet lined with parchment paper.
10. When the cake is done, remove it from the oven and let it cool in the pan for ten minutes. Then, carefully move the cake to a cooling rack. Put the crumbs sheet on top and bake for 15 minutes. Remove it and let it cool completely. Put it in a blender or food processor and pulse it a few times to make fine crumbs.
11. Once it has cooled enough, cut the cake in half horizontally for a single pan. Let it cook down. If you are in a hurry, put it in the fridge.

Prepare The Frosting:

1. In a large bowl, mix the powdered sugar and cream cheese. Use a medium-speed mixer to beat the mixture until it is smooth. Slow the mixer down to medium-low speed and pour the heavy cream down the side of the bowl in a steady stream. Use a silicone spatula to scrape the bottom and sides of the bowl every other time. Add the rest of the cream and turn the mixer to medium-high. Whip the frosting until it forms stiff peaks. If you are using vanilla extract, fold it and mix it with a spoon.
2. Put about 1.5 to 2 cups of the frosting into a piping bag with a big open star tip.
3. Add a few drops of ube flavor or color to the rest of the frosting and mix until combined. It doesn't have to be thoroughly combined, or you could over-beat the cream, turning it into butter. Move to a sewing bag with a flat, wide tip.

Assembly:

1. Place the cake plate or board on a cake rack. Place a small amount of the purple filling in the middle of the cake to hold it in place.
2. Position the cake's top, flat side down, in the middle of the plate. Put half of the white frosting from the middle ring outwards into it. After that, put the other half of the cake on top, with the cut side that looks better and is more even facing up.
3. Cover the sides with the ube filling by piping it from the bottom up as you turn the cake over. Include the top, too. It's not necessary to be perfect. Use a spoon to apply the frosting evenly to the cake.
4. Cover the whole cake with the cake bits.
5. Using the rest of the frosting, pipe some rosettes on top.

51. SANS RIVAL (LAYERED CASHEW CAKE)

Prep Time: 55 Minutes | Cook Time: 40 Minutes | Total Time: 1 Hour 35 Minutes | Serving: 12

Ingredients

For the meringue shells:

- ½ cup of roasted cashews
- 1 cup of sugar
- ¾ cups of ground roasted cashews
- ¼ cup of all-purpose flour
- 1 tsp cream of tartar
- 6 egg whites room temperature

For the buttercream frosting:

- ¼ cup of water
- 6 egg yolks
- 1/8 tsp vanilla extract
- 1 ½ cups of unsalted butter
- ¾ cup of sugar

For decoration:

- 1 cup of roasted cashew

Instructions

1. Preheat the oven to 300°F. Grease and flour four 8-inch round baking pans. Fill each pan with parchment paper and refrigerate.

To make the meringue shells:

1. Mix the flour, chopped cashews, and ground cashews in a bowl. Put away.
2. Put the egg whites and cream of tartar in a stand mixer bowl. Add the sugar one spoonful at a time, beating the mixture at medium speed. Speed up to medium-high and keep beating for about 4 minutes or until medium peaks form. Add a third of the flour mixture to the egg white mixture until it is well mixed.
3. Spread the batter evenly in the prepped pans, smoothing it with a spoon. Put the pans in the middle of the oven and bake for 40 minutes or until the meringue is golden brown.
4. Take it out of the oven. Right away, run a butter knife around the pan's sides and flip it onto a cooling rack to loosen the meringue shell. Remove the meringue shell from the parchment paper and set it aside to cool.

To make the buttercream frosting:

1. Put the egg whites in a stand mixer bowl. Whisk for about 5 minutes at medium speed until the color is pale. Put away.
2. In a small pot, mix the water & sugar. Set the pan on medium-high heat & let the sugar mix boil. Using a candy thermometer, monitor the syrup's temperature. Heat the sugar syrup until it reaches 240°F. Do not stir it. Remove the syrup from the heat & put it in a glass measuring cup.
3. After mixing the yolks on medium speed, slowly add the sugar syrup in a steady stream. Turn the mixer to medium-high and whisk for 8 to 10 minutes or until the yolk mixture cools. Last, make sure all the syrup is added. Whisk the mixture for about 20 seconds after adding butter, one cube

at a time. After you add the vanilla, whisk the mixture for another 5 minutes or until it is very smooth and silky.

To assemble the cake:

1. Put one meringue shell on a cake turntable. Place some frosting on top of the shell. Add the chopped roasted cashews on top. Put the last meringue shell on top to finish. Repeat the steps with the other two meringue shells. Spread the buttercream filling on top and sides of the cake. Add the chopped nuts on top. Put it in the fridge for at least two hours or overnight to set.

52. MANGO CAKE

Prep Time: 10 Minutes | Cook Time: 40 Minutes

Total Time: 50 Minutes | Serving: 8

Ingredients

- 1/4 cup of milk
- 1/4 tsp cardamom powder
- 1/2 cup of + 2 tbsp mango pulp
- 1/4 tsp baking soda
- 1 cup of flour
- 1/4 cup of oil
- 1 tsp baking powder
- 1/2 cup of sugar

Instructions

1. Put parchment paper around the edges of a 4x4-inch cake pan and oil them.
2. Put one cup of maida, one tsp of baking powder, and one-quarter tsp of baking soda into a bowl.
3. Make sure it's well mixed, then set it away.
4. Mix 1/4 cup of oil and 1/2 cup of sugar in a bowl.
5. Mix it well.
6. Put in 1/2 cup plus two tbsp of mango pulp.
7. Mix it well.
8. First, add 1/8 cup of milk. The milk needs to be boiled and at room temperature.
9. Mix it well.
10. Put a sieve over the bowl and pour the flour mixture into it.
11. Sort it out well.
12. Mix slowly.
13. Use a spoon to mix until no more dry flour is seen.
14. Now add the last 1/8 cup of milk. The milk needs to be boiled and at room temperature.
15. Slowly mix it until you have a smooth, creamy batter with no lumps.
16. Move the batter to the prepared cake pan. Tap it twice to remove any air bubbles.
17. With the oven already hot (180°C), bake the cake for 30 to 35 minutes or until a knife stuck in the middle comes out clean. Put it back in the oven for three to five more minutes if it's still sticky. Take the cake from the pan and let it cool for 5 to 10 minutes.
18. Then, use a knife to scrape the sides and flip the mold over to de-mold it.
19. Mango cake that is soft and tasty is ready!

53. NO BAKE YEMA CAKE

Prep Time: 20 Minutes | Cook Time: 20 Minutes | Total Time: 40 Minutes | Serving: 6

Ingredients

Dry:
- ½ tsp salt
- 1 cup of cake flour
- 2 tsp baking powder
- ¼ cup of granulated sugar

Meringue:
- 4 medium egg whites
- ¼ cup of granulated sugar

Wet:
1. 1 piece egg yolk
2. ½ cup of milk
3. ¼ cup of softened butter
4. 1 tsp vanilla extract

Yema Sauce:
1. 300 ml condensed milk
2. 370 ml evaporated milk
3. 250 ml all-purpose cream
4. 3 pieces egg yolks
5. 2 tbsp butter
6. 1 tbsp flour dissolved in ¼ cup of water

Toppings:
1. grated cheese

Instructions

1. Grease the llanera or pan with a little vegetable oil. If you're using a pan, put parchment paper on the bottom to make it easier to remove later. In a big bowl, mix the dry ingredients. Save for later.
2. Use a hand or stand mixer on low speed in a different big bowl to beat the egg whites until they foam up. Gradually add the sugar while beating the mixture until all the sugar is gone. Gradually increase the speed until hard peaks appear. Save for later.
3. Add the wet ingredients to the bowl with the dry ones, starting with the egg yolk and working your way around. Mix ¼ of the meringue into the batter using a whisk to make it lighter. In two or three additions or batches, fold the rest of the meringue into the batter. Just fold until you can't see any more white lines or lumps. Don't fold it too many times, or the meringue will lose its air.
4. Combine the ingredients and fill ¾ of the llanera or pan. Gently tap them to remove any air bubbles that are stuck inside.
5. They should be steamed over low heat for 15 to 20 minutes or until a toothpick stuck in them comes out clean. Put the llanera or pan on a rack for cooling. Once the cakes are cool enough to touch, use a knife to cut around the edges of the cake to remove it from its shape. Move the steamed cakes to serving plates or separate containers.
6. Make the yema sauce. Add evaporated, condensed, and egg whites to a deep skillet or saucepan. Mix slowly with a whisk. Over low heat, bring to a boil and stir often with a whisk so that the bottom doesn't burn. Keep stirring it as you add the heavy cream and flour mix until it gets thicker (but not too thick). After you turn off the heat, add the butter and mix it in well.
7. Place the cake on a plate, pouring yema sauce over it. Sprinkle with grated cheese.

54. CHOCOLATE CRINKLES

Prep Time: 15 Minutes | Cook Time: 10 Minutes

Total Time: 25 Minutes | Serving: 20

Ingredients

- 2 large eggs
- 1 cup of granulated sugar
- 1 tsp vanilla extract
- 1 cup of all purpose flour
- 1 tsp baking powder
- 1/2 cup of confectioners sugar
- 1/2 cup of cocoa powder
- 1/4 tsp salt
- 1/4 cup of vegetable oil

Instructions

1. Put the cocoa powder, oil, vanilla extract, eggs, and granulated sugar in a mixing bowl. Whisk the ingredients together until they are perfectly smooth.
2. Mix the flour, baking powder, and salt in a different bowl.
3. Stir the flour mixture into the cocoa mixture after adding it.
4. Put the dough in the fridge for at least three to twelve hours.
5. Turn the oven on to 350°F. Divide the dough evenly into 20 cookies using a small ice cream scoop. Then, wet your hands and roll each cookie into a ball the same size. Coat each ball in powdered sugar.
6. Place the cookies on a baking sheet, leaving room between each one. Depending on size, they should be baked for 10 to 12 minutes. After baking, the cookies will harden.
7. Let the cookies cool down a bit. Place them on a wire rack to cool completely afterward.

55. PIANONO (SPONGE CAKE ROLL)

Prep Time: 20 Minutes | Cook Time: 20 Minutes | Total Time: 35 Minutes | Serving: 6

Ingredients

- 5 large egg whites
- 1/4 tsp baking powder
- 3/4 cup of all-purpose flour
- 3/4 cup of granulated sugar
- 1 tsp vanilla
- 5 large egg yolks
- 1/4 tsp kosher salt
- 1/2 cup of granulated sugar
- 1/4 cup of powdered sugar
- 1/2 tsp cream of tartar

Filling Options:

- Coconut jam
- Your favorite jam
- 1 stick butter/margarine traditional and sugar
- Ube Halaya

Instructions

1. Preheat the oven to 375°F with a rack placed in the center. To prepare the pan, put butter-covered parchment paper on both sides of a 9x13-inch jelly roll pan. Make sure the paper goes all the way around the pan. Cutting holes in the corners will help it fit better. Put away.
2. Mix the eggs, vanilla, and 3/4 cup of sugar in a big bowl. Add the flour, baking powder, and salt and mix until well combined. Put away. Beat the egg whites until they are foamy in a clean glass bowl or the clean bowl of an electric mixer with the whisk attachment. Start on low speed to break up the whites. When you add the cream of tartar, whisk it in until it gets bigger. Add the 1/2 cup of sugar in tbsp by tbsp , and raise the speed to medium until the egg whites form soft peaks. When you flip your whisk over, the meringue will start to hold together, and the peak will drop and droop. This means that the meringue has hit soft peaks.
3. Fold about half a cup of the meringue slowly into the batter to make it softer and more spread. Once this is all mixed, fold the rest of the meringue into the batter in three parts. Use a flick and wiggle of the wrist to gently fold the meringue into the batter without overmixing it and making it lose air. Using an offset spoon, spread the batter out evenly in the jelly pan that has been prepared.
4. The cake should be golden in a 13–15-minute bake, and a knife stuck in the middle should come out clean. Take the cake out of the oven and drop it from a height of 1" onto a wire rack. This will help keep the cake from shrinking.
5. Wait five minutes and then touch the cake. Put powdered sugar on the cake once it's cool enough to touch. Spread butter on a second piece of parchment paper and place it on top of the meringue, butter side down. Place a light cutting board or baking sheet on top, then flip the cake onto a work area. Remove the top piece of parchment paper from the jelly roll pan. Cut one of the short sides at a 45-degree angle to make it look better. This will let the cake roll rest properly with the seam side down. Wrap the warm cake carefully around the parchment paper on the bottom. Start rolling from the short end that hasn't been cut. The seam side should be down on a wire rack. Leave it at room temperature for about an hour or until cool.
6. To fill the cake, gently unroll it and use an offset spoon to spread it out, leaving a 1/2-inch border around the edge. If you need to, add a little more filling to the ends of the cake before rolling it back up. Put it back in the buttered paper and let it rest if you won't serve it immediately.
7. The length of time you give the cake to rest or chill will depend on the filling you choose. You can serve right away if you use regular sugar, melted margarine, or butter. Before you put jam, custard, or whipped cream inside, put the cake in the fridge for at least 4 hours or overnight.
8. Cut off the ends of the cake roll before serving for a cleaner look. Sprinkle the cake roll with powdered sugar, cut it into pieces, and serve.

56. MAMON (SPONGE CAKE)

Prep Time: 35 Minutes | Cook Time: 25 Minutes

Total Time: 1 Hour | Serving: 12

Ingredients

- 100 g cream cheese
- 7 egg whites
- 7 egg yolks
- 1 cup of sugar
- 2 tbsp canola oil
- ¼ tsp lemon juice
- 3/4 tsp baking powder
- ½ cup of milk
- 1 cup of cake flour
- 70 g butter

Instructions

1. Add three to four inches of boiling water to a pot. After boiling the water, turn down the heat and let it cook slowly. Put the cream cheese, butter, milk, and olive oil in a heat-safe glass bowl. Put the glass bowl on top of the pot of boiling water. The bowl should fit properly over the pot. The water that is slowly cooking shouldn't reach the bowl's bottom. Should it, you should carefully lower the amount of water. The mixture will be smooth after the butter and cream cheese have melted, so whisk it occasionally. Give it time to cool down.
2. Add the egg whites and mix the whole thing with a whisk to make it smooth.
3. The flour and baking powder should be sifted over the egg yolk mixture. Combine till smooth. Heat the oven to 350°F.
4. Whip the egg whites until they are foamy with a stand or hand mixer. While mixing, add the lemon juice and keep going until soft peaks form. Little by little, add the sugar until stiff peaks form.
5. Little by little, add ⅓ of the egg whites at a time and mix them into the egg yolk mixture. The finished mixture's color should be the same all over.
6. Use 12 big muffin tins to put the batter into.
7. Arrange the cups of in a big baking or roasting pan with a lip. Place the pan in a hot 350F oven. As you slowly pour water into the roasting pan, make sure that the mamon shapes are only 1/3 of the way submerged.
8. Put it in the oven for 25 to 30 minutes or until a toothpick stuck in the middle comes out clean. Abandon the oven. Just barely open the oven door, and let the mamon sit inside for three minutes. Remove from the cups of and let cool on a wire rack. You can take them out of the cups of before serving if you want.

57. ENSAYMADA (SWEET BRIOCHE)

Prep Time: 3 hours 20 minutes | Cook Time: 35 minutes

Total Time: 3 hours 55 minutes | Serving: 16

Ingredients

- ¼ cup of butter
- 1 cup of milk
- ⅓ cup of sugar
- 3 egg yolks
- ½ cup of shortening
- 1 envelope active dry yeast
- 3 ½ cup of flour
- ¼ tbsp salt

TOPPINGS:

- ½ cup of powdered sugar
- 1 cup of Kraft cheese
- ½ cup of butter

Instructions

1. Mix milk, butter, sugar, and salt in a bowl.
2. Add half of the flour and the yeast that has grown. Mix on medium speed for three to five minutes or until the dough turns into a paste.
3. Mix in the egg whites and the rest of the flour for three more minutes. If the mix is too wet or sticky, add more flour, but not too much. Sticky is what the dough should be like.
4. Scrape the sides of the bowl as you fold the dough in the middle. Cover with a kitchen towel. Rest and rise in a warm place for two to three hours or until it has grown twice as big.
5. As you flip the sticky dough over to the lightly floured work surface, scrape the sides of the bowl.
6. Make a ball out of the dough and cut it in half. Roll each log and cut it in half again. Do this again and again until you have 16 slices.
7. Make a rectangle out of a slice about 8 inches by 4 inches with a rolling pin. Spread melted butter on top of the rectangle. Roll it from one end of the long side to the other to make a long, thin log. Then, tuck one end under and roll it into a circle.
8. Put each coil of dough in a greased mold and let it rise in a warm place for thirty minutes to an hour or until it's almost twice as big.
9. Set the oven to 300°F and bake them for 20 to 25 minutes. After baking, let them cool for a few minutes before removing them from the pans. Then, let them cool down.
10. Mix ½ cup of melted butter and ½ cup of powdered sugar to make the buttercream.
11. With a knife or spoon, spread buttercream on top of the ensaymadas and sprinkle with a lot of chopped cheese.

58. CREMA DE FRUTA CAKE

Prep Time: 20 Minutes | Cook Time: 35 Minutes | Total Time: 55 Minutes | Serving: 8

Ingredients

- 2 tbsp unflavored gelatin
- 8 pieces egg yolks
- 1 3/4 cups of sugar
- 1/3 cup of butter
- 1 1/2 tsp vanilla extract
- 2 1/4 cups of water
- 1 1/2 cup of flour
- 1 tsp baking powder
- 1 big can fruit cocktail
- 4 cups of milk

Instructions

1. Mix the baking powder and 1 cup of flour for the sponge cake using a flour sifter. Put away
2. In a mixing bowl, add four egg whites and beat them until the mixture gets thick.
3. Slowly add 1/2 cup of sugar while beating the egg.
4. As you go, slowly add the sifted flour and baking powder mix. Thoroughly mix the items.
5. Mix 1 cup of milk, butter, and vanilla extract in a saucepan. Then, cook until the butter melts.
6. Add the cooked mixture (milk, butter, and vanilla extract) to the mixing bowl and mix it with the other ingredients until evenly distributed.
7. Warm the oven up to 350°F.
8. Mix the ingredients and pour them into a baking pan. Bake for 23 minutes or until the sponge cake is done. Put away.
9. Warm up a pot and add 1/4 cup of sugar to it. This will make the simple syrup.
10. Add 1/4 cup of water immediately and cook until the sugar is gone. Then, let it cool for a few minutes.
11. Put the simple syrup on the sponge cake and then spread it out. (I used a brush to spread the syrup)
12. Mix 1/2 cup of flour, 1 cup of sugar, and 3 cups of milk in a pot to make the custard. Cook while stirring the mixture until it thickens.
13. Add half of the cooked mixture to the bowl with the egg yolks and mix it well.
14. Add the rest of the items to the saucepan with everything else. This is now the custard. Mix until the thickness is thick enough.
15. Spread the custard layer out evenly on top of the sponge cake.
16. Take the fruit cocktail out of the liquid concentrate and set it away.
17. Lay out all of the fruits on top of the custard. Arrange them in a sensible way.
18. Mix two cups of water with the gelatin.
19. Melt the gelatin and fruit cocktail concentrate in a pot. Then add hot water and bring to a boil.
20. When it starts to boil, remove it from the heat and let it cool until slightly warmer than room temperature.
21. Place the layer of gelatin on top of the fruit drink.
22. Put in the fridge (ideally overnight).
23. Serve chilled for dessert.

59. SYLVANAS (CASHEW MERINGUE WITH BUTTERCREAM)

Prep Time: 1 Hour 30 Minutes | Cook Time: 40 Minutes

Total Time: 2 Hours 10 Minutes | Serving: 20

Ingredients

For the Dacquoise:

- 1 1/2 cups of cashew
- 1 tsp vanilla
- 6 egg whites
- 3/4 cup of granulated sugar
- a pinch of cream of tartar

For the Buttercream:

- 1/4 cup water
- 2 cups of unsalted butter
- 6 egg yolks
- 1 tsp vanilla
- 1 cup sugar

To Garnish:

- 3/4 cup of ground cashew

Instructions

For the Dacquoise:

1. Set up a cookie sheet with parchment paper and a plain-tipped pipe bag.
2. To make the meringue, use a bowl without oil. Beat the egg whites and add a pinch of cream of tartar. Once they form soft peaks, add the sugar slowly and then the vanilla. Keep beating until you get stiff peaks.
3. When you carefully fold in the chopped cashews, be careful not to deflate the meringue. Put the meringue into a plain-tipped pipe bag. You can also use a ziplock bag and cut off one corner to make a simple tip.
4. Use a 1.5 to 2-inch diameter pipe, or use the already-made guide.
5. After 20 to 30 minutes at 325F, it should be golden brown.
6. Let it cool down before adding the frosting.

For the buttercream:

1. Prepare a small pot, a stand mixer (easier to use) with a wire whisk attachment, and a candy thermometer.
2. Add sugar and water to a small pot and stir to mix. Warm up the stove a bit so that the syrup can boil.

3. The egg whites should be put in the bowl of your stand mixer while you wait for the syrup to reach 240F. At medium speed, beat the eggs with the wire whisk tool until they become lighter in color and thicker.
4. Take the sugar syrup off the stove when it reaches 240F.
5. Add the syrup to the beaten egg whites. While beating the egg whites constantly, slowly add the sugar in a steady stream.
6. Once all the sugar is mixed in, keep whipping at medium-high speed until the food is cool. Feel the bottom of the bowl to see if it's still warm. If it is, keep whipping it. After the mixture has cooled down enough, add the butter.
7. Start adding butter, about one to two squares or cubes at a time, while the mixer is still medium-high. Make sure to mix well after each addition. Do this again and again until all the butter is mixed in.
8. Switch out the wire whisk attachment for the paddle attachment on your stand mixer. Then, add the vanilla. Keep beating the buttercream until it's very soft and smooth.

Putting It All Together:

1. Turn the flat side out to get a smooth, even top and bottom. Place a cookie dacquoise between two pieces of paper and spread frosting on one side.
2. Buttercream should be put on the top and sides. Putting the frosting in the fridge for 20 minutes will make it easier to work with before you add it to the bottom.
3. Roll the cookies in ground cashews after covering them with frosting.
4. Cool cookies down; they taste best that way.

FRIED & BAKED DESSERTS

60. PIYAYA (FLATBREAD WITH MOLASSES)

Prep Time: 15 Minutes | Cook Time: 5 Minutes | Total Time: 20 Minutes | Serving: 4

Ingredients

- ½ tsp salt
- 1 – 2 tbsp sesame seeds
- 3 tbsp muscovado sugar
- ½ tbsp granulated sugar
- 4 – 5 tbsp ice cold water
- 1 cup of all-purpose flour
- 3 tbsp cold unsalted butter

Instructions

1. Mix the flour, salt, and sugar in a medium-sized bowl. When you add the raw butter, use your fingers, a fork, or a pastry cutter to mix it into the flour. Use your fingers because this is a small amount of dough. Sprinkle the ice water over the flour mixture and mix it well. If the dough is too wet, add more flour. If it's too dry, add more water.
2. Spread out on a clean surface dusted with more flour. Knead the dough until smooth to form a flat ball. Cut the dough into six pieces with a regular or cutting knife. Make a ball out of a piece. Press each piece into a circle with your fingers, like you're making a dumpling. This will make a small well. Add half a tbsp of muscovado sugar and close it up by pinching the sides. Make a ball again and press it down with your hand. Get a small rolling pin and make the piaya as flat as you can. It should be about 3 to 4 inches across. Make sure there aren't any holes. Pinch them shut if you find any. The muscovado will leak out if you don't. Put sesame seeds on both sides and press down to make it stick. Turn on medium heat and heat a big cast iron or nonstick pan. Carefully place the piayas in the pan. Cook for three minutes on each side or until they turn golden brown.

61. CAMOTE CUE (CARAMELIZED SWEET POTATOES)

Prep Time: 10 Minutes | Cook Time: 15 Minutes

Total Time: 25 Minutes | Serving: 4

Ingredients

- 1 pound sweet potatoes
- 1 cup of brown sugar
- 2 cups of vegetable oil

Instructions

1. Use a knife or peeler to clean and peel the sweet potatoes. Cut into slices that are half an inch thick. Put away. Warm the oil over medium heat. Add half of the brown sugar and wait for it to melt and float to the top of the oil. Slowly add slices of camote or sweet potato to the hot oil.
2. Use a spoon to move the pieces around the pan and cover them with caramel.
3. Let it fry for a while. Cover the camote pieces with the remaining sugar and keep frying them until they turn golden brown. Take it out of the oil and let it cool down a bit.
4. Put three to four pieces on separate bamboo sticks.
5. Serve and enjoy.

62. BANANA FRITTERS (MARUYA)

Prep Time: 10 Minutes | Cook Time: 15 Minutes | Total Time: 25 Minutes | Serving: 6

Ingredients

- cooking oil
- ¼ cup of sugar
- 6 pieces Saba Banana ripe

Batter:

- 1 tsp salt
- ¾ cup of flour
- 1 tsp baking powder
- ¼ cup of cornstarch
- ½ cup of water or milk
- ¼ cup of granulated sugar

Instructions

1. Use a masher to break the bananas into small pieces in a big bowl. Be careful not to make them too mushy, as you want the marula to have body and texture. You could also slice or split them.
2. Put all the dry ingredients in a bowl and mix them. Add the milk and mix with a spatula until everything is mixed. It doesn't matter if there are a few lumps. It will be hard to spread.
3. Mix the mashed bananas into the batter with a spatula until everything is well mixed.
4. Heat oil in a pan over medium heat. Add a small amount of the mixture to the hot oil, using a spoon to flatten it. Add three to four scoops of the mix to the pan.
5. Fry both sides until they turn brown. Using a pair of spoons, roll the cooked Maruya in sugar.
6. Serve while still warm.

63. BAKED BIBINGKA

Prep Time: 10 Minutes | Cook Time: 35 Minutes | Total Time: 45 Minutes | Serving: 3

Ingredients

- 1/4 cup of milk
- 2 1/2 tsp baking powder
- 1 cup of rice flour
- 1/2 cup of granulated sugar
- 1/8 tsp salt
- 1/4 cup of coconut
- 3 pieces raw eggs
- Pre-cut banana leaf
- 1 cup of coconut milk
- 1 piece salted duck egg sliced
- 3 tbsp butter
- 1/2 cup of cheese

Instructions

1. Warm the oven up to 375°F. Mix the salt, baking powder, and rice flour well. Put away.
2. After beating the butter, add the sugar slowly while stirring. Then add the eggs and whisk until all the ingredients are well mixed. Add the rice flour, salt, and baking powder mixture slowly while mixing. Add the fresh and coconut milk, and then whisk some more for one to two minutes.
3. Place the banana leaf already cut in a bake or cake pan. Spread the mix out on the pan.
4. Set the oven to 150°F. Take it out of the oven and add the sliced salted egg and chopped cheese. Do not turn off the oven yet. Put it back in the oven and bake for another 20 minutes or until the top is a mild brown color. Take it out of the oven and let it cool down.
5. Cover in butter and sprinkle coconut flakes on top. Serve and enjoy!

64. CARIOCA (FRIED GLUTINOUS RICE BALLS)

Prep Time: 15 Minutes | Cook Time: 25 Minutes | Total Time: 40 Minutes | Serving: 4

Ingredients

For the Rice balls:

- oil for frying
- ½ cup of water
- 1 cup of glutinous rice flour

For the Sugar Syrup:

- 1 cup of sugar
- ¼ cup of water

Instructions

1. Mix sticky rice flour and water in a bowl until a dough forms.Make a ball out of a tbsp of the dough. Do the same for the rest of the dough. Poke holes in the balls keep them from breaking too much when fried.Put oil in a pan or dish and set it on medium or low heat.
2. If you need to, fry the balls one at a time. To make sure they cook evenly, turn them every so often. They are done when they turn light gold and double in size.Put the carioca balls out of the hot oil on a rack lined with paper towels to cool.Mix the sugar and water in a pot to make the caramel syrup. Stir it around until the sugar is gone. Warm it up slowly until it starts to bubble.
3. Drop the heat and add the rice balls to the pan. Stir the balls slowly to ensure they are covered in sauce all around.Make bamboo sticks out of the rice balls and serve them!

65. BAKED PUTO

Prep Time: 10 Minutes | Cook Time: 35 Minutes | Total Time: 45 Minutes | Serving: 5

Ingredients

- 1 ½ cups of all-purpose flour
- 1 tbsp. + 1 tsp. baking powder
- 1 cup of milk, whole milk
- 2 tbsp. water
- slices of cheese or salted duck egg for toppings
- 3/4 cup of sugar
- 2 tbsp unsalted butter
- 2 eggs
- 1/4 tsp Pandan essence (optional)

Instructions

1. Place a 1" thick baking tray or a large roasting pan that would fit a muffin tray on the top rack of the oven. Once the tray is full of warm water, preheat the oven to 325°F.
2. Place the eggs in a medium-sized bowl and beat them. Next, add the milk, sugar, and melted butter. If you use Pandan essence, mix it with the water before adding the eggs. If you have an electronic mixer, mix the eggs on low speed until they are well mixed. Mix the egg and milk, then add the sorted flour and baking powder. Fold the mixture in, and then beat on low again.
3. Fill about two-thirds of each muffin tray cup with batter. You don't have to grease the pan, but you can put paper cups in it if you want to. The muffin tin should go on top of the sheet or pan of hot water on the oven's upper rack. The water should be boiling. Bake in the oven with steam for 20 minutes or until a toothpick comes out dry.
4. Place a piece of salted duck egg on top of each Puto cup before putting them in the oven. After they're baked, put a piece of quick-melt cheese, like Velveeta or Swiss, on top of each Puto, and then put the muffin tray back in the oven for one to two minutes. At this point, you can turn off the oven.
5. Turn off the oven and let the tray cool for five minutes. Carefully lift each puto cup off the tray with a rubber spatula and serve.

66. PINEAPPLE UPSIDE-DOWN CAKE

Prep Time: 25 Minutes | Cook Time: 45 Minutes | Total Time: 1 Hour 10 Minutes | Serving: 8

Ingredients

Topping:

- 8–10 pineapple slices
- 1/4 cup of unsalted butter
- 1/2 cup of packed light
- 15–20 maraschino cherries

Cake:

- 1/3 cup of sour cream
- 6 tbsp unsalted butter
- 3/4 cup of granulated sugar
- 2 tbsp milk
- 2 large egg whites
- 1 tsp baking powder
- 1 tsp pure vanilla extract
- 1/4 cup of pineapple juice
- 1 and 1/2 cups of
- 1/4 tsp baking soda
- 1/2 tsp salt

Instructions

1. Warm the oven up to 350°F. Put 1/4 cup of melted butter into a 9-by-2-inch pie dish or round cake pan that hasn't been oiled. Spread the brown sugar over the butter. Use a clean or paper towel to soak up any extra liquid on the fruit. Put 6-7 pineapple slices blotched and all the cherries on top of the brown sugar. While you make the cake batter, put the pan in the fridge for a few minutes. This helps the topping's design stay in place. Mix the baking powder, soda, salt, & cake flour with a whisk. Put away. At high speed, use a hand mixer with whisk tool to beat the butter for about one minute until it is smooth and creamy. After adding the sugar, it will take about a minute to beat on high speed until the mixture is smooth. If you need to, use a wooden spatula to scrape the sides and bottom of the bowl. Add the egg whites and beat on high speed until they are well mixed in. Add the sour cream and vanilla extract and beat again. When you need to, scrape the bowl's sides and bottom. Mix the dry ingredients with the wet ones. Place the mixer on low speed. Slowly add the pineapple juice and milk while the mixer is running. Just beat on low speed until all the ingredients are mixed. Do not mix too much. To make sure there are no lumps at the bottom of the bowl, you might have to whisk it all by hand. The batter is going to be a little thick. Take the topping out of the fridge. Pour cake batter over the topping and spread it out evenly. Bake the cake for 43 to 48 minutes, covering it with foil halfway through baking so the top doesn't get too brown before the middle is fully cooked. It is done when you stick a toothpick into the middle of the cake, and it mostly comes out clean. A few moist bits are fine. Should your cake take longer to bake or rise & stick to the foil, don't worry. Take the cake out of the oven and let it cool for 20 minutes on a wire rack. Turn the cake over onto a cake stand or serving plate after it cools. It's okay if some of the topping juices run off the sides. The cake can be served warm, but they will be messy. Before cutting and serving, I think it's best to let the cake cool to room temperature. Do not put the cake in the fridge to cool it down faster; it might taste too thick if you do. Cover extra slices & put them in the fridge for up to three days or the freezer for up to three months. Let it thaw at room temperature. If you want to freeze the cake as a whole, don't do it. The toppings don't thaw very well. See below for how to get ahead.

67. CHEESE ENSAYMADA

Prep Time: 45 Minutes | Cook Time: 20 Minutes

Total Time: 1 Hour 5 Minutes | Serving: 16

Ingredients

- 1 cup of milk
- 1 envelope active dry yeast
- ½ cup of shortening
- ¼ cup of butter
- 3 egg yolks
- ¼ tbsp salt
- ⅓ cup of sugar
- 3 ½ cup of flour

Toppings:

- 1 cup of Kraft cheese
- ½ cup of butter
- ½ cup of powdered sugar

Instructions

1. Mix milk, butter, sugar, and salt in a bowl.
2. Add half of the flour and the yeast that has grown. Mix on medium speed for three to five minutes or until the dough turns into a paste.
3. Mix in the egg whites and the rest of the flour for three more minutes. If the mix is too wet or sticky, add more flour, but not too much. Sticky is what the dough should be like.
4. Scrape the sides of the bowl as you fold the dough in the middle. Cover with a kitchen towel. Rest and rise in a warm place for two to three hours or until it has grown twice as big.
5. As you flip the sticky dough over to the lightly floured work surface, scrape the sides of the bowl.
6. Make a ball out of the dough and cut it in half. Roll each log and cut it in half again. Do this again and again until you have 16 slices.
7. Make a rectangle out of a slice about 8 inches by 4 inches with a rolling pin. Spread melted butter on top of the rectangle. Roll it from one end of the long side to the other to make a long, thin log. Then, tuck one end under and roll it into a circle.
8. Put each coil of dough in a greased mold and let it rise in a warm place for thirty minutes to an hour or until it's almost twice as big.
9. Set the oven to 300°F and bake them for 20 to 25 minutes. After baking, let them cool for a few minutes before removing them from the pans. Then, let them cool down.
10. Mix ½ cup of melted butter and ½ cup of powdered sugar to make the buttercream.
11. With a knife or spoon, spread buttercream on top of the ensaymadas and sprinkle with a lot of chopped cheese.

68. PAN DE COCO (COCONUT BREAD)

Prep Time: 15 Minutes | Cook Time: 20 Minutes

Total Time: 35 Minutes | Serving: 12

Ingredients

Dough:

- 1 tsp instant dry yeast
- ¼ tsp salt
- ¾ cup of lukewarm milk
- 2 cups of all-purpose flour
- ⅓ cup of sugar
- ¼ cup of vegetable oil

For the Filling:

- ½ cup of water
- ½ cup of brown sugar
- 1 ½ cup of coconut
- 2 tbsp butter
- 1 tsp vanilla extract -optional

.For the Egg Wash:

- 1 small egg
- 1 tbsp water

Instructions

Prepare the Dough:

1. In a large bowl, sift together the flour, sugar, and salt in a large bowl. Then add the quick dry yeast and mix it in.
2. Add the wet ingredients. Mix them with a wooden spoon or spatula until they form a dough.
3. Place the dough on a flat surface and work it around. Put oil on your hands and the surface to keep the dough from sticking if it is too wet or sticky. Add more oil to the dough if it's too dry. The dough should become less sticky and easier to work with as you knead it. If you add more flour, the rolls might get too thick. Based on many things, it could take as little as 7 minutes or as long as an hour. To be sure, do the windowpane test.
4. Cover the dough with plastic wrap or a clean dish towel and put it in a greased bowl. Let it rise for 30 minutes to an hour or until it's almost twice as big as before.

Filling:

1. While you wait, prepare the filling. Heat water in a pan over medium-low. Mix in the brown sugar and butter, then let it cook until it becomes thick.

2. Add the chopped coconut and cook for a few minutes until the syrup is completely absorbed. Don't heat the filling anymore; let it cool down.
3. Forming and Assembly:
4. Roll the dough out flat by gently punching it down. To make it flat, flip it over. Cut each piece of dough in half lengthwise for 12 pieces. Then, cut crosswise into four equal pieces. Form a ball out of each piece. The dough pieces should rest for at least three to five minutes after they are done.
5. Press down on each piece of dough with your hands. Put a tbsp of coconut filling in the middle of the flattened dough and hold it in the curve of your palm.
6. Roll it between your hands to make it round again, then pinch the corners together to fully enclose the filling.
7. Place the dough disks one inch apart on a baking sheet lined with parchment paper. Lightly press them down to make the buns flatter.
8. Fork-hole each filled dough ball in the middle. In 20 to 30 minutes, or until they double in size, cover them with a clean kitchen towel and let them rest again.

Egg Wash:

1. Combine 1 egg and 1 tbsp of water and beat until frothy. Set aside.

Baking:

1. Set the oven to 325°F and bake for 10 minutes. After taking it out of the oven, brush egg wash on the baking pan with the buns. Put the buns back in the oven and bake for five more minutes until they turn golden brown.
2. Take the buns out of the oven and let them cool before serving them. Enjoy with a cup of coffee or tea.

69. PINIPIG CRUNCH

Prep Time: 15 Minutes | Cook Time: 5 Minutes

Total Time: 20 Minutes | Serving: 6

Ingredients

Vanilla Cream:

- ½ cup of milk powder
- ½ tsp vanilla extract
- 1 ½ tbsp cornstarch
- ¼ cup of sugar
- ¼ cup of milk
- 1 cup of whole milk

Chocolate Shell:

- ⅔ cup of coconut oil
- 1 cup of pinipig
- ½ cup of powdered sugar
- ½ cup of cocoa powder
- ½ cup of milk powder - optional

Instructions

1. Mix the slurry in a small bowl by adding the cornstarch and ¼ cup of milk. Put away.
2. Put sugar and powdered milk in a pot and mix them with a whisk. Slowly add the whole milk while stirring to break up the sugar and powdered milk.
3. Set the mixture on medium heat and stir it around a few times. As you pour in the slurry, keep stirring to prevent it from getting lumpy. You should cook it until it starts to get thicker, but it should still be easy to pour, like ice cream that has broken down.
4. Take it off the heat, add the vanilla extract, and mix it in. After letting it cool, pour it into ice-drop shapes. Cover each mold with aluminum foil and cut a small hole in the top to make putting an ice cream stick in easy.
5. Put it in the freezer for at least four hours or overnight.
6. Combine all the ingredients for the chocolate magic shell and mix until smooth. Transfer the mixture to a tall, thin glass.
7. While the ice cream is still cold, use an ice drop to dip the mold in warm water. This will help the ice cream come off the mold more easily.
8. Put the pork on a plate and spread the vanilla ice cream flat to cover it. Then, flip it over and do the same thing on the other side.
9. Place a vanilla ice drop covered in piña into the chocolate mixture and dip it in. Then, lift it out of the chocolate. You can dip it three or four times for a thick cover. Hold it up for a moment to make the shell harder. If you want, you can also add more pinipig while the chocolate is still soft.
10. You can serve it right away, wrap it in foil or plastic, and freeze it to enjoy later.

70. UBE CHEESE PANDESAL

Prep Time: 30 Minutes | Cook Time: 20 Minutes

Total Time: 50 Minutes | Serving: 14

Ingredients

- 3 ½ cups of flour
- 1 packet active dry yeast
- ½ cup of bread crumbs
- ½ pound Velvetta cheese
- ¼ cup of warm milk
- ½ cup of mashed ube
- 6 tbsp white granulated sugar
- 1 tbsp vegetable oil
- 3 tbsp butter
- 1 tsp salt
- ¼ cup of warm water
- 2 eggs, lightly beaten
- 1 ½ tbsp liquid ube flavoring

Instructions

1. Put 105°F to 110°F warm water in a mixing bowl. Add the active dry yeast and one tbsp of sugar to the water. Let the mix sit for about 5 minutes or until it foams up.
2. After the butter has melted, mix the eggs, the rest of the sugar, the mashed purple yam, ube flavoring, and salt with a wooden spoon.
3. Each time you add a cup of flour, stir the dough well so that it turns into a messy mass. You may not need to use the whole ½ cup of leftover flour. Add enough to keep the dough from sticking together and stir until it forms a ball in the middle of the bowl.
4. Put a little oil on a rolling board and take the dough out.
5. Lightly oil your hands, and then knead the dough by pressing it down and away from your body with the heels of your fingers. Do this until the dough is smooth and elastic but still a little sticky.
6. Cover the dough with a dish towel and put it in a lightly greased bowl. Let it rise for about an hour and a half to two hours or until it doubles in size.
7. From the risen dough, make a 20—to 22-inch log. To make 14 pieces, cut the log in half vertically and then into seven smaller pieces from each half.
8. Spread each piece of dough with your palms and put a piece of cheese in the middle. Wrap the cheese in the dough and roll it into a smooth ball. Tuck the ends under to seal.
9. Spread the dough on a baking sheet lined with parchment paper in a single layer, about ½ inch apart. Roll the dough in bread crumbs.
10. Lay it out on a clean kitchen towel and cover it lightly. Let it rise for 30 to 60 minutes or until it puffs up and doubles.
11. Warm the oven up to 350 F.
12. Put it in the oven for 20–23 minutes. Remove it from the oven and let it cool down a bit. The filling will be hot.

71. COCONUT MACAROONS

Prep Time: 20 Minutes | Cook Time: 20 Minutes

Total Time: 40 Minutes | Serving: 24

Ingredients

- 1 tsp vanilla extract
- 6 ounces semi-sweet chocolate chips
- ⅔ cup of sweetened condensed milk
- 2 large egg whites
- ½ tsp salt
- 1 bag sweetened coconut

Instructions

1. Warm the oven up to 325°F. Put parchment paper around the edges of two baking sheets.
2. Mix the coconut, sweetened condensed milk, vanilla, and salt in a big bowl.
3. Set the egg whites in a second, bigger bowl. Beat them at high speed for about 3 minutes or until stiff peaks form. Add the egg whites to the coconut mixture and mix them in.
4. Using a ½- tbsp ice cream scoop, put cookie dough on the baking sheets lined up, leaving about 1 inch of space between each.
5. Put one sheet in the oven at a time and bake for 20 to 25 minutes or until the sides and tops are golden brown. Let it cool on the pan.
6. Put the semisweet chocolate in a bowl that can go in the microwave. Stir the chocolate every 15 to 30 seconds in the microwave on high until it's smooth and melted.
7. Use the chocolate to cover the bottom of the warm cookies. Put them back on the baking sheets lined with foil and let them cool to room temperature. If you don't want to dip the cookies, drizzle the chocolate over them. Cookies can be kept at room temperature for up to a week in a container that keeps air out.

TRADITIONAL FILIPINO CANDIES

72. PASTILLAS DE UBE (PURPLE YAM MILK CANDIES)

Prep Time: 20 Minutes | Cook Time: 40 Minutes | Total Time: 1 Hour | Serving: 4

Ingredients

- 16 ounces boiled ube
- 1 can Ube-flavored condensed milk
- 1 cup of Mochiko sweet rice flour
- 2 tsp McCormick Ube flavoring
- 1/2 cup of granulated sugar

For wrappers:

- 20 pieces clear cellophane wrappers

Instructions

1. Make sure the frozen, boiled purple yam has thawed at room temperature. Do not put it in the microwave to thaw.
2. Put the ube, the condensed milk that tastes like ube, the rice flour, and the ube flavoring in a big bowl. Mix the liquid well with a big wooden spoon until it is smooth and there are no lumps. Put away.
3. Get the steamer ready. Fill the bottom pot three-quarters of the way to the top with water. With the lid on, let the water boil over medium-high heat.
4. Before using the round baking pan, spray its bottom and sides with cooking spray. Spoon the ube mix into the pan.
5. Place the pan with the ube inside the second layer of the steamer. Then, put this layer on the pot with hot water at the bottom.
6. Cover the ube mix and cook it for an hour.
7. After an hour, take the ube out of the oven and use the tip of a sharp knife to poke a hole in the middle to see if it's done. To make ube, cut a knife almost all the way through and make sure it feels hard.
8. Take the round pan out of the steamer. After letting it cool on the counter, put it in the fridge for about 30 minutes. This will firm it up and make it easier to shape into balls.
9. To get the Pastillas de Ube ready and wrap them up
10. Take the ube paste that has been cooked out of the fridge.
11. Using a spoon and your (pre-greased) hands, form the ube balls into soft treats 1 inch across.
12. Sprinkle sugar on each ball and roll it in it. Cover all of the pastillas with sugar.
13. You can use clear cellophane wrapping to protect each ube pastilla if you want to. For the pastillas to stay sealed, tightly twist the ends of the wrapper together.
14. Put the ube pastillas in the fridge to keep them fresh. It can last up to three weeks.

73. POLVORON (TOASTED MILK CRUMBLE)

Prep Time: 10 Minutes | Cook Time: 20 Minutes

Total Time: 30 Minutes | Serving: 40

Ingredients

- 1 cup of powdered full cream milk
- 1 cup of sugar
- 1 cup of butter
- 2 cups of flour

For the Pinipig Flavor:

- ½ cup of pinipig

For the Cashew or Peanut Flavor:

- ½ cup of unsalted cashew or peanut

For the Cookies and Cream Flavor:

- 6 Oreo cookies
- 1 tbsp butter

Instructions

1. Put flour in a pan set on medium heat. Toast it, turning it often, until it's lightly browned and smells good. Remove it from the heat and let it cool.
2. Whisk the powdered milk, sugar, and toasted flour until well mixed. Add the butter and keep stirring until well mixed.
3. Put the mixture in a flat baking dish, and then use a Polvoron mold to make it into solid cookies. Mold should be packed down as much as possible.
4. Spread out in a single layer on a baking sheet. Freeze for about 30 minutes or until hard.
5. Put each one in its own cellophane or Japanese paper bag.

For the Pinipig Flavor:

1. Put the pinipig in a pan over medium-low heat. Toast it, turning it often, until it turns a little brown and starts to pop. Remove it from the pan and let it cool.
2. Use a food processor to grind the ingredients into a coarse powder.
3. Add to the polvoron mix with a whisk until everything is well mixed.

For the Cashew or Peanut Flavor:

1. Put cashews or peanuts in a pan over medium-low heat. Toast, turning often, until the food smells good. Remove the pan from the heat and let it cool.
2. Use a food processor to grind the ingredients into a coarse powder.
3. Add to the polvoron mix with a whisk until everything is well mixed.

For the Cookies and Cream Flavor:

1. Take the cream filling off of the cookies.
2. Use a food processor to grind the ingredients into a coarse powder.
3. Add a tbsp of butter to the polvoron mixture and mix well with a whisk.

74. YEMA BALLS (CUSTARD CANDY BALLS)

Prep Time: 10 Minutes | Cook Time: 20 Minutes

Total Time: 30 Minutes | Serving: 30

Ingredients
- 2 tbsp unsalted butter
- sugar
- 3 pieces egg yolks
- oil or baking spray
- 1 10- ounce can condensed milk
- pinch salt

Instructions
1. Put butter in a pan and melt it over low heat.
2. Stir in the condensed milk until everything is well mixed.
3. Add egg whites and salt. Stir the mixture for about 20 minutes until it becomes very thick.
4. Put the mixture on a plate or clean, lightly greased surface. Let it cool down.
5. Take a tsp of the yema mix and roll it into a ball. Cover in sugar, then serve.

75. PEANUT BRITTLE

Prep Time: 5 Minutes | Cook Time: 20 Minutes

Total Time: 25 Minutes | Serving: 50

Ingredients
- 2 cups of sugar
- 1 cup of light corn syrup
- 1/2 cup of water
- 1 1/2 tsp vanilla
- 2 cups of salted roasted peanuts
- 2 tbsp butter
- 1 1/2 tsp soda

Instructions
1. Put parchment paper on the bottom of a sheet pan. Put away.
2. Prepare by measuring the peanuts, butter, baking soda, and vanilla.
3. Put water and sugar in a medium-sized pot and stir them together well. Add the corn syrup and mix it in. Don't raise the heat! Stir the mixture now and then as you cook it over medium heat until it comes to a soft boil.
4. Put the candy thermometer on the pot's edge, ensuring it's in the liquid but not touching the bottom. Cook, stirring occasionally, until the temperature reaches 250°F.
5. Add the peanuts and stir the mixture when the candy thermometer reads 300°F.
6. Take the mixture off the heat and immediately add the butter, baking soda, and vanilla. It will foam and change consistency.
7. When the pan is ready, carefully pour the hot mixture onto it. Then, use a knife or spoon to spread the mixture into an even layer quickly.
8. Let it cool completely (at least 30 minutes) before breaking it up and eating it.
9. Once the peanut brittle has fully cooled, put it in a container that won't let air in.

76. COCONUT JAM (MATAMIS NA BAO)

Prep Time: 5 Minutes | Cook Time: 40 Minutes

Total Time: 45 Minutes | Serving: 0

Ingredients

- 1 cup of muscovado sugar
- salt
- 2 cans coconut cream
- ¼ tsp pandan extract optional

Instructions

1. Put coconut cream in a pot and bring it to a boil. Keep boiling until soft curds form.
2. Put in the pandan extract, sugar, and salt.
3. Slowly cook it over medium-low heat until it gets thick.
4. Take it off the heat and let it cool down.
5. Serve right away or transfer to a jar that has been sterilized.

77. PANUTSA (PEANUT BRITTLE WITH MOLASSES)

Prep Time: 15 Minutes | Cook Time: 20 Minutes

Total Time: 35 Minutes | Serving: 4

Ingredients

- 1 tsp Baking Soda
- 3 cup of pecans, walnuts, or peanuts
- 1/2 cup of water
- 2 cup of granulated sugar
- 1 cup of Molasses
- 1 cup of butter

Instructions

1. Prepare two 13x9x2-inch baking pans by buttering them up well.
2. Mix the sugar, molasses, and water in a big saucepan.
3. Stir the sugar mixture over medium-low heat until the sugar melts. Bring to a boil, then add the butter and mix well.
4. When the syrup hits the thread stage around 230°F, stir it often.
5. Add the nuts when the temperature reaches 280°F, known as the "soft-crack stage."
6. Constantly stir until the hard-crack stage, which is 300°F.
7. Take it off the heat and quickly mix in the baking soda. Mix well. Pour into baking pans that have been prepped.
8. As the brittle cools, use forks to lift and pull at the edges to make it thinner.
9. Take the candy out of the pans and flip it over as soon as possible.
10. Break up hardened candy and put it in a jar that won't let air in.

78. ESPASOL (RICE FLOUR AND COCONUT LOGS)

Prep Time: 30 Minutes | Cook Time: 30 Minutes | Total Time: 1 Hour | Serving: 35

Ingredients

- 16 ounce glutinous rice flour
- 2 14- ounce cans coconut milk
- 1 10- ounce can condensed milk
- pinch salt
- 1 12- ounce can evaporated milk

Instructions

1. Toast the glutinous rice flour in a large pan or wok over medium-high heat. Stir it often to prevent burning. Take it off the heat when it turns a light brown and smells good.
2. Keep about ½ cup of the toasted flour away. Cover the bottom of your pan with half of that amount. Don't eat the other part yet.Put all the ingredients, including the rest of the toasted flour, in a big bowl and mix them until well combined.Put it back in the pan and heat it. Use a mesh sieve to remove the lumps.Turn down the heat to medium-low and stir the mixture until it becomes a ball. Watch the blend carefully so it doesn't catch fire.
3. When the mixture is smooth and shiny, remove it from the heat and pour it into the prepared pan. Spread it out evenly.Cover with the rest of the flour that you set aside to toast. Cover the whole surface.Let it cool down a bit, then cut it up and serve. You can cover each piece with more toasted flour if you want to.

79. BUKAYO (SWEET COCONUT STRIPS)

Prep Time: 5 Minutes | Cook Time: 20 Minutes

Total Time: 25 Minutes | Serving: 6

Ingredients

- ¼ cup of coconut water or just plain water
- 2 cups of coconut strings from young coconut
- 1 ½ cups of brown sugar

Instructions

1. Warm up a nonstick pan and add coconut water. Slowly mix the two until the coconut water becomes a thick sauce.
2. Add the coconut strings and mix them until the syrup fully covers them. Let it cook on low heat until the syrup thins out and gets even thicker.
3. When the syrup thickens, remove the pan from the heat and set it on the counter with a trivet or hot stand under it.
4. Hold off until the syrup stops fizzing and becomes a little less hot. Then, keep stirring the mixture until it melts and turns clear as it becomes thick and sticky.
5. Put some of the mixture on top of a banana leaf. Shape into a round, flat ball, and repeat with the rest of the dough.
6. Let it cool down all the way and set, then carefully take them off the banana leaves.
7. Move to a serving plate or a jar with a lid to store.

80. YEMA BARS

Prep Time: 15 Minutes | Cook Time: 30 Minutes

Total Time: 45 Minutes | Serving: 30

Ingredients

- 3 pieces egg yolks
- 1 10- ounce can condensed milk
- pinch salt
- sugar
- 2 tbsp unsalted butter
- oil or baking spray

Instructions

1. Put butter in a pan and melt it over low heat.
2. Stir in the condensed milk until everything is well mixed.
3. Add egg whites and salt. Stir the mixture for about 20 minutes until it becomes very thick.
4. Place the mixture on a plate or lightly greased clean surface. Let it cool completely.
5. Take a tsp of the yema mix and roll it into a ball. Cover in sugar, then serve.

81. MACAPUNO BALLS (COCONUT CANDIES)

Prep Time: 10 Minutes | Cook Time: 10 Minutes

Total Time: 20 Minutes | Serving: 35

Ingredients

- Skimmed milk
- 1 cup of cornstarch
- 1 ½ cup of macapuno preserves
- 1 cup of water
- 1 small can condense milk

Instructions

1. Drain the macapuno preserve through a fine-mesh sieve or colander. Add 2 cups of water to remove some of the thick syrup.
2. Mix the cornstarch and water in a pot, whisking well to break up the cornstarch. Add the macapuno and condensed milk to the mix.
3. Stir the food while cooking over medium-low heat until it thickens. Stir the mixture often while cooking until it comes from the pan and turns into a sticky dough. Remove it from the heat and let it cool down.
4. After the dough has cooled, grease your hands with oil to prevent it from sticking. Take about a tbsp of dough and shape it into balls.
5. Put skim milk powder on a different plate. Roll the balls in the powdered milk to cover them.
6. Wrap each in a different paper color or small boxes or bags.

82. PASTILLAS DE LECHE

Prep Time: 30 Minutes | Cook Time: 30 Minutes | Total Time: 1 Hour | Serving: 40

Ingredients

- 4 cups of carabao's milk
- ½-3/4 cup of powdered milk
- Caster sugar for rolling
- 6 tbsp caster sugar
- 1 tbsp butter

For Wrapping:

- 40 pieces 2x3-inch white paper
- 40 pieces 3x5-inch tissue or Japanese paper

Instructions

1. Pour new milk into a large pan. Heat it until it starts to cook. Let it cook on low heat for 15 minutes, turning it often. Add the sugar and mix until it's all mixed in. To keep the mixture from burning, stir it constantly with a wooden spoon, scraping the bottom as you go.
2. Keep cooking the mixture until it has shrunk and turned into a thick paste. Lower the heat and add the butter. Mix well. (Take the pan off the heat.) Add the powdered milk and mix it in until a sticky dough forms. Let the milk dough cool down fully before moving it to a plate or bowl.
3. Make a cylinder shape with the milk dough and cut it into four equal pieces. Roll a piece of it into a smaller log. Then, cut the log into ten similar pieces. Create a roll for every piece that is about ½ inch long. Cover all of each piece with white sugar by rolling it in it.
4. Put a small piece of white paper in the middle of a piece of pastillas and wrap it around it, leaving both ends open. Wrap them both in tissue paper. Push the extra tissue paper from the ends inwards to cover the holes.

83. COCONUT TAFFY

Prep Time: 10 Minutes | Cook Time: 15 Minutes | Total Time: 25 Minutes | Serving: 16

Ingredients

- 8 grams Cashew Nut Powder
- ¼ tsp Ground Cardamom
- ½ cup of Water
- ¼ tsp Salt
- 4 grams Milk Powder
- 180 grams Desiccated Coconut
- 290 grams White Granulated Sugar
- 2 tbsp Rose Water
- 1-2 drops Gel Food Colour

Instructions

1. Put parchment paper around the edges of an 8x8-inch cake pan.
2. Mix the milk powder, cashew nut powder, salt, and dried coconut in a medium-sized bowl for a short time.Put the sugar, water, and rose water in a cool pot. The sugar should melt without stirring while the stove is on medium heat. If you need to, move the pot around every once in a while. The melted sugar syrup should reach a temperature of 235°F, about the same as a baseball. It's also possible to drop a spoonful of sugar syrup into a bowl of ice water and see if it makes a string at the bottom. If it does, the sugar syrup is ready.Add the food coloring and mix it with the sugar syrup until the color is well mixed.Mix in the cardamom powder and the mix of dried coconut. Do this for about one to two minutes until the coconut has soaked up all the tasty flavors.Before you know it, the coconut candy will be thick enough to eat. Pour it into the prepared cake pan. Let it cool a bit before making small marks on the pieces of coconut toffee.
3. Brush some butter on a sharp knife, and once the coconut toffee has cooled completely, cut it into pieces.Add a dot of royal icing and a silver bead to the top to make the coconut candy look nice.

COOKIES & BISCUITS

84. LENGUA DE GATO (BUTTER COOKIES)

Prep Time: 30 Minutes | Cook Time: 15 Minutes

Total Time: 45 Minutes | Serving: 60

Ingredients

- 1 tsp vanilla extract
- 2 pcs egg whites
- ½ cup of granulated sugar
- ½ cup of unsalted butter
- pinch salt
- 1 cup of all-purpose flour

Instructions

1. Warm the oven up to 350°F. Put parchment paper on two baking sheets or cookie trays and set them aside.
2. With an electric hand mixer or a stand mixer with a paddle attachment, beat ½ cup of butter in a large bowl on medium-high speed for two to three minutes until it is soft and smooth.
3. You should keep beating it for another 4 to 5 minutes after adding the last ½ cup of sugar. Do not forget to scrape the bowl's sides and bottom.
4. Add egg whites and one tsp of vanilla extract. Beat until everything is mixed in (4-5 minutes).
5. Turn the speed down to low and slowly add 1 cup of flour and a pinch of salt until everything is mixed.
6. Place the cookie dough in a sewing bag or a Ziploc bag with a tip cut off so that it is about ½ inch wide.
7. Fill your baking sheets with dough and pipe 3-inch-long cookies on them, leaving about an inch of room between them.
8. Bake the lengua de gato for 12 to 15 minutes or until the sides are lightly browned and the center is dry.
9. Remove the pans from the oven and let the cookies cool a bit in them. Once the time is up, move the parchment paper to a cooling rack and let the lengua de gato cool down. Remove the cookies from the parchment paper, then eat them.

85. OTAP (PUFF PASTRY BISCUIT)

Prep Time: 25 Minutes | Cook Time: 35 Minutes | Total Time: 1 Hour | Serving: 50

Ingredients

For the dough:

- 2 tsp vanilla extract
- 35 grams sugar
- 1 tsp salt
- 16 grams lard
- 320 grams all-purpose flour
- 32 grams self-rising flour
- ¾ cup of water

For the filling:

- 1 tsp vanilla extract
- 5 tbsp all-purpose flour
- 1 tsp baking powder
- ¼ cup of lard
- 2 tbsp vegetable oil

For coating:

- ½ cup all-purpose flour
- 2 tbsp brown sugar
- ½ cup white sugar

Instructions

Making the dough:

1. Mix all-purpose flour, self-rising flour, sugar, and salt in a bowl.
2. Whisk in the water and vanilla extract until they are fully mixed in.
3. Knead the dough with your hands until it comes together. Then add the lard and knead some more until the dough is smooth and sticky. A stand mixer can also help you do this faster and easier. Roll the dough into a ball. Place the dough-filled mixing bowl under a clean kitchen towel and set it aside for at least 5 minutes.

Making the filling:

1. Mix vegetable oil, baking powder, vanilla extract, and lard in a small mixing bowl.
2. Add the all-purpose flour and mix it in with a whisk until it's smooth and the flour is gone.
3. Putting together and cutting dough Put the dough on a clean work surface greased with oil. Roll it out flat until it's about 24 inches long and 16 inches wide. Cover all of the dough with the filling. Add 1/2 cup of flour to the top of the filling and make sure it covers everything. Roll the dough into a log slowly, starting from the end closest to you. Cut the dough log in half to make it easy to handle, then oil both sides. You'll see that the inside has a spiral pattern. To make a spiral, turn a piece of cut dough over so the spiral path faces up. Run it through a rolling pin until it's 4 inches long, 2 inches wide, and oval-shaped. Do the same thing with the rest of the dough.

Coating and baking:

1. Mix brown and white sugar in a large bowl. Be generous and cover both sides of the tap.
2. Place the covered tap on a baking sheet lined with parchment paper. Set the oven to 356°F and bake for 35 minutes or until golden.

86. ROSQUILLOS (RINGLET COOKIES)

Prep Time: 5 Minutes | Cook Time: 15 Minutes

Total Time: 20 Minutes | Serving: 30

Ingredients

- 0.11 ounce Baking Soda
- 6.17 ounce Sugar
- 0.04 ounce Bakels Baking Powder
- 0.88 ounce Egg White
- 2.47 ounce Egg Yolk
- 5.29 ounce Soft Flour
- 0.04 ounce Salt
- 1.06 ounce Vegetable Oil
- 1.06 ounce Bakels Baking Powder
- 3.53 ounce Cake Flour

Instructions

1. Use a paddle to mix Bakels Margarine Special, oil, sugar, and baking soda at a medium speed.
2. Put in egg yolks and egg whites. Keep mixing until the salt and sugar are gone.
3. Mix Fino double-acting baking powder and flour. Add little by little to the bowl mixture. Mix well on low speed, but don't mix too much.
4. Put the mix on a floured work surface. Use a mosquito cutter to cut the cookie dough into circles about 1/4 cm thick. Place the circles on a lightly greased baking sheet.
5. Place in the oven and bake at 180°C for 20 to 25 minutes or until done.

87. BROAS (LADYFINGERS)

Prep Time: 15 Minutes | Cook Time: 10 Minutes

Total Time: 25 Minutes | Serving: 12

Ingredients

- ½ tsp salt
- ½ cup of confectioner's sugar
- ⅔ cup of all purpose flour
- 3 egg whites
- 3 egg yolks
- ½ tsp vanilla

Instructions

1. Warm the oven up to 325°F. Mix the flour and salt. Put away.
2. Beat the egg yolk in a bowl.
3. Slowly add the sugar while beating the egg whites until stiff. Then, add the vanilla.
4. Along with the egg whites, fold the egg yolk in.
5. Slowly add the flour mix after that.
6. Use a spoon to scoop the batter and shape it into a 3-inch log on a greased baking sheet.
7. Put it in the oven for 8 to 10 minutes or until the edges turn brown.

88. BISCOCHITOS TRADITIONAL COOKIES

Prep Time: 20 Minutes | Cook Time: 10 Minutes

Total Time: 30 Minutes | Serving: 72

Ingredients

- 2 large eggs
- ¼ tsp salt
- 6 cups of all-purpose flour
- 1 tbsp ground cinnamon
- 2 cups of lard
- 1 ½ cups of white sugar
- 2 tsp anise seed
- 1 tbsp baking powder
- ¼ cup of white sugar
- ¼ cup of brandy

Instructions

1. Turn the oven on to 350°F. Put the baking powder, flour, and salt in a bowl that has been sifted.
2. Mix lard and 1 ½ cups of sugar in a big bowl using an electric mixer until smooth. Beat in the anise seed until the mixture is light and fluffy. Add the eggs one at a time and mix well. Mix the flour and brandy to make a dough.
3. Use a floured rolling pin to make the dough 1/4 to 1/2 inch thick. Cut the dough into shapes like fleur-de-lis or something else easy. Place cookies that have not been oiled on baking sheets. In a small bowl, mix 1/4 cup of sugar and cinnamon. Then, sprinkle this mixture over the cookies.
4. Baking in a hot oven will take about 10 minutes until the edges are golden brown.

89. PINEAPPLE COOKIES

Prep Time: 10 Minutes | Cook Time: 20 Minutes

Total Time: 30 Minutes | Serving: 20

Ingredients

Pineapple Cookies:

- 2 cups of all purpose flour
- 4 ounce . cream cheese
- ¾ cup of granulated sugar
- 1 large egg
- 1 tsp vanilla extract
- ¼ cup of light brown sugar
- ½ cup of pineapple
- ½ tsp salt
- 1 tsp baking powder
- ½ cup of unsalted butter
- 1 tbsp pineapple juice

Pineapple Glaze:

- 1½ cups of powdered sugar
- 2 - 3 tbsp pineapple juice

Instructions

1. Add the flour, baking powder, and salt to a bowl and mix them using a whisk.
2. Put the crushed pineapple in a different bowl and drain it. Save ¼ to ⅓ cup of the pineapple juice to use in both the cookies and the glaze. Leave alone for now.
3. Use an electric hand mixer with beaters or a stand mixer with a paddle attachment to cream the butter and cream cheese until smooth and well mixed. On average speed, this takes two minutes. Clean the bowl's sides and bottom.
4. For another two minutes, cream the butter and cream cheese mixture with the light brown and granulated sugars on medium speed. Add the egg, vanilla extract, and pineapple juice and mix on low speed until smooth and well mixed.
5. Add the dry ingredients to the wet ones just until they are mixed. Add the drained, crushed pineapple and mix it in. Put the dough in the fridge with the lid on for 30 to 60 minutes or overnight.
6. While the cookies chill, warm the oven to 350°F. Place parchment paper on two large baking sheets.
7. Put 1½ to 2 tbsp of the cookie dough on the prepared baking sheet. I like to use a small cookie scoop to get cookies that are just the right size.
8. Bake the sugar cookies with pineapple glaze for 13 to 15 minutes. The bottoms of the cookies will be a very light golden brown color.
9. Take the cookies out of the oven and cool them on a rack. After 4 to 5 minutes, remove them from the hot baking sheet and put them on the rack to cool until they are at room temperature.
10. Make the pineapple glaze for the pineapple drop cookies by mixing 1½ cups of powdered sugar with 2 to 3 tbsp of the pineapple juice you saved.
11. Put some pineapple sauce on top of every cookie. Let the cookies set for about an hour, then eat them.

90. UBE CRINKLES

Prep Time: 15 Minutes | Cook Time: 30 Minutes

Total Time: 45 Minutes | Serving: 20

Ingredients

- 2 cups of all-purpose flour
- 2 pcs large eggs beaten
- 7 ounce ube jam or ube halaya
- ½ cup of granulated sugar
- ½ cup of canola oil or vegetable oil
- 1 cup of confectioner's sugar
- 3 tsp ube extract
- ½ tsp salt
- 2 tsp baking powder

Instructions

1. Mix the flour, baking powder, and salt in a medium bowl. Put away.
2. Using an electric hand mixer or a stand mixer with a paddle tool, mix the oil, granulated sugar, and ube jam (ube halaya) until they are all mixed together. At this point, you should taste the blend to see if it needs more sugar. Ube jams are different, so you must make changes based on your taste.
3. Once you're happy with the taste, add beaten eggs and ube flavor. Mix everything.
4. In thirds, add the flour mixture to the ube mixture and stir slowly on low speed until everything is mixed. Make sure each addition is mixed in, and don't forget to scrape the bowl's sides and bottom.
5. Put the bowl of cookie dough in the fridge for at least 4 hours with the plastic wrap on top.
6. When you're ready, set the oven to 350°F. Prepare a baking sheet with parchment paper (or plastic baking mats) and put it away.
7. Take a big tbsp of ube cookie dough and roll it into a ball with your hands. Before putting each ball on the cookie sheet, cover it completely with confectioner's sugar. Leave about one to two inches between each cookie.
8. Put them in a hot oven for 10 to 13 minutes or until the tops crack and look dry. Don't worry if they are soft when they come out of the oven; they will set as they cool. Just make sure you don't bake them too long.
9. Allow to cool in the pan for a few minutes before moving to a rack to finish cooling.

91. ALMOND COOKIES

Prep Time: 10 Minutes | Cook Time: 10 Minutes

Total Time: 20 Minutes | Serving: 12

Ingredients

- 1 ½ cups of all-purpose flour
- ½ tsp baking soda
- ½ tsp vanilla extract
- ½ tsp almond extract
- ½ cup of unsalted butter
- ½ tsp cream of tartar
- ¼ tsp table salt
- 1 large egg
- ¾ cup of powdered sugar
- ½ cup of sliced almonds plus more for topping

Instructions

1. Warm the oven to 350°F. Line a cookie sheet with parchment paper if you like.
2. Put ½ cup of sliced almonds in a mixer or food processor. You can also chop by hand. Chop or pulse until the food is broken into small, pebble-like pieces of different sizes. Put away.
3. Melt the butter and powdered sugar in a low-speed bowl with an electric mixer. Beat for about one minute until the mixture is light and fluffy.
4. It will take about 30 seconds to mix the egg, vanilla extract, and almond extract well.
5. The dry ingredients are flour, cream of tartar, baking soda, and salt. Put them in a separate bowl and mix them with a whisk. Add the milk slowly, about ½ cup at a time, until everything is well mixed. Add the ground nuts and mix well.
6. The dough will be slightly wetter than usual, but that's okay. Still, it should be easy to shape into balls about the size of a full tbsp.
7. Put them in a bowl of powdered sugar and toss them around to coat. Then, put them on a baking sheet lined with parchment paper. Space the cookies 2 inches apart. If you want, you can add some sliced nuts to each cookie's top.
8. Put the cookies in the oven at 350F for 9 to 11 minutes, or until they look puffy and set around the sides.
9. Remove it from the oven and let it rest for two to three minutes before moving it to a rack to cool. Enjoy!

92. PUTO SEKO (RICE FLOUR COOKIES)

Prep Time: 10 Minutes | Cook Time: 15 Minutes | Total Time: 25 Minutes | Serving: 12

Ingredients

- ¼ cup of Softened Butter
- ⅓ cup of Condensed Milk
- 1 cup of Cornstarch

Instructions

1. Preheat the oven to 325°F before you start. A moderate heat level is best for the Puto Seko since you don't want it to burn or brown. Remove the water.
2. Blend all the ingredients together in a food processor until a nice, hard, and soft dough appears, about one to two minutes.
3. Unless you have a food processor, you can do this all by hand. It will take about 10 minutes of mixing and then hand-doing to get the same texture.
4. Put parchment paper on a baking sheet. Place the dough on the prepared baking sheet. Use a food mold to scoop out the dough.
5. For fifteen minutes, bake it. Then, turn off the heat and prop up the oven door with a wooden spoon. For cool and dry, leave the Puto Seko inside.
6. Take it out of the oven once it is completely cool.
7. Do not touch the cookies easily; they should sound hollow when you tap them.

93. SPANISH BREAD COOKIES

Prep Time: 15 Minutes | Cook Time: 25 Minutes

Total Time: 40 Minutes | Serving: 24

Ingredients

- Pinch salt
- 2 tsp. cinnamon
- 2 cup of sugar
- 1 cup of butter
- 1/2 pound . almonds with skins
- 2 eggs
- 3 cup of flour
- 2 tsp. cloves

Instructions

1. Mix sugar and butter. Beat in the eggs. Add the flour, cinnamon, cloves, and salt. Put in almond flour. Roll it up, put it in the fridge, cut it up, and bake it at 350°F for 10 to 12 minutes until it turns brown. The next day is best.

94. PEANUT COOKIES

Prep Time: 5 Minutes | Cook Time: 15 Minutes

Total Time: 20 Minutes | Serving: 18

Ingredients

- 1/2 cup of butter
- 1/2 cup of sugar
- 1 cup of peanut butter
- 1 1/2 cup of all-purpose flour
- 1 egg large
- 1 tsp vanilla extract 5mL
- 1/2 cup of brown sugar
- 3/4 tsp baking powder

Instructions

1. Heat the oven to 350°F.
2. You can sift the flour and baking powder together, then use a whisk to mix them.
3. Cream the butter and sugars in a stand mixer with a paddle attachment. If you like, add 1/4 to 1/2 tsp of sea salt.
4. Add the peanut butter and mix it in until it's all mixed in.
5. Once the egg and vanilla extract are mixed, add the flour mixture and beat it until it's well combined.
6. Roll the dough into balls about an inch in diameter on a baking sheet lined with parchment paper.
7. Use a fork to make a crisscross design in the cookies.
8. Put the cookies in the oven for 10 minutes.
9. Let cookies cool down on the baking sheet; they need time to set up before they can be moved.

JELLY &GELATIN DESSERTS

95. BUKO PANDAN GELATIN

Prep Time: 10 Minutes | Cook Time: 20 Minutes | Total Time: 30 Minutes | Serving: 8

Ingredients

- 2 cups of sugar
- 4 cups of coconut juice
- 2 ½ cups of coconut milk
- 1 package agar-agar bars
- 3 drops buko pandan flavor extract
- 1 cup of young coconut

Instructions

1. Cut the agar bars into little bits.
2. Soak the agar in coconut juice in a big pot for about 30 minutes or until it becomes soft.
3. Bring to a boil over medium heat and stir until the agar-agar melts.
4. After adding the sugar, stir the food often and cook for another 10 to 15 minutes.
5. Pandan extract, coconut milk, and chopped young coconut should all be added. Stir it to ensure the color is spread out. Bring to a simmer, but DO NOT BOIL. Continue cooking for two to three minutes until everything is hot. Take the liquid off the heat and put it in a lightly greased 8- cup of gelatin mold. As it cools, the gelatin will start to set.
6. Put it in the fridge for about an hour or two or until it's completely set.
7. Carefully flip the dish onto a serving plate and cut it into serving sizes.

96. COFFEE JELLY

Prep Time: 5 Minutes | Cook Time: 5 Minutes | Total Time: 10 Minutes | Serving: 4

Ingredients

- 10 grams gelatin powder
- 2 cups of medium to strong coffee
- 4 tbsp granulated sugar
- Milk, heavy cream, or whipped cream, for topping (optional)

Instructions

1. Mix two tbsp of cold water with the gelatin powder in a bowl. Put away.
2. Bring the water to a boil and add the sugar and instant coffee to a bowl. You could heat the coffee until it's hot, pour it into a bowl, and add the sugar.
3. After you add the gelatin, whisk it in until it's all gone.
4. Put the jelly in 4 small cups of , cover with a lid or plastic wrap, and refrigerate for 3 to 4 hours or until set.
5. Serve it as is, or drizzle a little milk or heavy cream on top, or add a dollop of whipped cream.

97. CATHEDRAL WINDOW GELATIN

Prep Time: 4 Hours | Cook Time: 5 Minutes | Total Time: 4 Hours 5 Minutes | Serving: 5

Ingredients

- 1 1/2 cup of gelatin red, yellow, and green jelly
- 4 packets unflavored gelatin
- 1 can condensed milk
- 1 1/2 cups of pineapple juice
- 1 1/4 cups of whipping cream

Instructions

1. Heat the pineapple juice in the microwave oven for 35 seconds.
2. Put it in a bowl for mixing. Add the gelatin that is clear and has no taste. Push and stir the gelatin into the juice until fully mixed in.
3. Add the condensed milk to the bowl after adding the heavy cream. Mix everything well.
4. Put in the colored pieces of jelly. Mix.
5. Put the mix into a Jelly shape that is big enough to hold everything.
6. Put in the fridge for 4 hours.
7. Move the food to a plate. Cut and serve.

98. MANGO GELATIN WITH CREAM

Prep Time: 15 Minutes | Cook Time: 10 Minutes | Total Time: 25 Minutes | Serving: 8

Ingredients

- 1 Can Evaporated Milk
- 1 Can Table Cream Crema Mexicana
- 4 Ripe Mangoes
- 10 tsp Unflavored Gelatin
- 1/2 cup of Whole Milk
- 1 Can Condensed Milk
- 1/2 cup of water
- 1 box Cream Cheese

Instructions

1. Add the plain gelatin to the water in a bowl and mix it well. Take a 15-minute break.
2. Cut the mangoes into cubes that are about the size of a pencil.
3. Put the whole milk and mangoes in a blender and blend them. The mixture will be a little thick.
4. Put the mango mixture from above into a medium-sized pan. Heat it over medium-low heat for five minutes, being careful not to let it boil. After 5 minutes, turn down the heat to the lowest setting possible.
5. To turn the gelatin mixture back into a liquid, heat the bowl with the plain gelatin for about 30 seconds.
6. When you add the gelatin mixture to the mango mixture in the pan, stir it until it's all melted. Remove it from the heat and let it cool.
7. Use a mixer to mix the cream cheese, evaporated milk, condensed milk, and table cream.
8. After adding the mango mixture, mix it well. Pour it into a big bundt pan and refrigerate for at least three to four hours.

99. GULAMAN (AGAR-AGAR)

Prep Time: 20 Minutes | Cook Time: 30 Minutes | Total Time: 50 Minutes | Serving: 4

Ingredients

- 1 packet gulaman powder or bar

Instructions

Using Gulaman Powder:

1. Prepare the gulaman powder by mixing it with cold water or another liquid, like fruit juice. Using less liquid gives the powder a stronger texture.
2. Stir the mixture constantly over medium-high heat until it dissolves completely. Using plain gulaman, you can add taste boosters like pandan leaves or vanilla extract. If needed, add sugar.
3. If any bits haven't dissolved, strain the mixture into a mold.
4. Before cutting it up and serving, set it at room temperature or in the fridge.

Using Gulaman Bar:

1. Tear or cut the bar into smaller pieces to help it break down faster.
2. Put in enough water or another liquid to cover the gulaman.
3. Soak the gulaman for about 30 minutes to soften and rehydrate it. Some brands might not need to be soaked first; check the packaging for exact guidelines.
4. While stirring, bring the mixture to a boil over medium-high heat. If the gulaman lacks flavor, add pandan or vanilla to improve its taste, and add sugar as needed.
5. Strain the mixture to get rid of any bits that aren't dissolved.
6. You can put the mixture in the fridge to speed up the process or set it at room temperature. After it has set, you can cut or release the gulaman into the desired shape.

100. PANDAN JELLY WITH COCONUT MILK

Prep Time: 15 Minutes | Cook Time: 45 Minutes | Total Time: 1 Hour | Serving: 6

Ingredients

For The Pandan Layer:

- 3.5 cups of water divided into 3 cups of and 1/2 cup of
- 8 pandan leaves
- 1/2 cup of white sugar
- 1 tbsp agar-agar powder

For The Coconut Layer::

- 1 tbsp agar-agar powder
- 1/2 cup of water
- 1 tsp salt
- 2 cups of coconut milk
- 1/2 cup of white sugar

Instructions

For Pandan Layer:

1. Mix the agar-agar powder and 1/2 cup of water well in a small bowl. Wait 15 minutes before using it.
2. Thai basil leaves should be cut into 1-inch pieces.
3. Add the rest of the water to a blender along with the sliced pandan leaves and blend them roughly.
4. Pour the fresh pandan juice into a bowl. Use cheesecloth to catch the leaves that have been mixed in. Using a smaller filter will make it easier to paint with pandan.
5. Heat the strained pandan juice in a wok, skillet, or cooking pot for one minute over low to medium heat. Then, add the agar-agar mix from step 1, but not before stirring it again.
6. Cook and stir for 5 minutes until the agar-agar powder is gone. Before proceeding, the agar must be 100% broken down. Check the back of a spoon to see if there are still agar traces.
7. The sugar should be added after the agar-agar has been broken down. Stir and cook some more until the sugar is gone.
8. Pour or scoop the pandan layer into a bowl, baking dish, or cup. Be careful not to break the pandan layer. It will get firmer if you leave it at room temperature for about 30 minutes.

For Coconut Layer:

1. Put the coconut on top. As in step 1, stir agar-agar and 1/2 cup water in a bowl. Take a 15-minute break.
2. After 15 minutes, put the coconut milk in a pan or pot and slowly cook it over low to medium heat. Add the agar mix when the edges start to bubble. Allow it to cook for no more than 5 minutes or until the agar-agar powder is fully mixed in.
3. Add the sugar and salt. Cook for two minutes, until the sugar is completely melted, then remove the pan from the heat.
4. Check with your finger to see if layer 1 is firmer. Once it's hard, add the smooth coconut mixture in layers with a big spoon.

5. Put the treat on the counter and let it sit for 30 minutes. After that, you can eat it immediately or put it in the fridge to enjoy later when it's cold.

101. SAGO AT GULAMAN (TAPIOCA AND JELLY DESSERT)

Prep Time: 5 Minutes | Cook Time: 25 Minutes | Total Time: 30 Minutes | Serving: 6

Ingredients

- 1 cup of tapioca pearls
- 2 tbsp granulated white sugar
- 6 cups of water
- 1/2 ounce red gelatin powder

Syrup:

- 1 cup of brown sugar
- 1 tsp vanilla extract
- 1 cup of water

Instructions

1. Cook the tapioca by boiling 4 cups of water in a pot. Add the pieces of tapioca. Set the heat to medium and boil for eight minutes. Turn down the heat to its lowest level and keep boiling until the pearls become clear and chewy. Leave it alone.
2. Boil 2 cups of water in a pot to cook the gelatin. Add the gelatin powder and white sugar. Remove the mixture from the heat and mix it. Transfer the mixture to a glass jar. Wait for it to cool. Refrigerate the mixture until it sets.
3. Mix all the ingredients for the sauce in a cooking pot. Bring it to a boil. Stir for one minute while cooking. Remove from heat and put away.
4. In a glass, mix sliced gelatin, tapioca pearls, three tbsp of syrup, and a cup of cold water.
5. Serve and enjoy!

102. LYCHEE GELATIN

Prep Time: 4 Hours 30 Minutes | Total Time: 4 Hours 30 Minutes | Serving: 4

Ingredients

- 500 g lychee
- 50 g sugar
- 5 sheets white gelatin
- 2 sheets red gelatin
- 3 tbsp lemon juice

Instructions

1. Drain the lychee from the can, then mix the fruit and liquid with sugar and lemon. Let it sit for an hour.
2. Warm up some cold water and add gelatin to it. Add lychee juice to 1/2 L (about 2 cups of) of water and heat it just a bit. Squeeze the gelatin well, then stir it into the lychee juice.
3. After adding half a lychee fruit to the gelatin mixture, place four small ring molds in the fridge to set. Before serving, quickly dip the molds in hot water. Then, take the gelatin out of the molds and spread the remaining lychee fruits in the middle of the gelatin.

103. RAINBOW GELATIN

Prep Time: 1 Hours 30 Minutes | Total Time: 1 Hours 30 Minutes | Serving: 10

Ingredients

Rainbow Gelatin Layers:
- 2 cups of juice
- 3 1/2 tsp unflavored gelatin

White Gelatin Layers:
- 1 1/2 cans condensed milk
- 7 1/2 tsp unflavored gelatin
- water

Instructions

1. Prepare a 9-by-13-inch baking sheet with a lip for the Rainbow Jello.
2. Put one cup of juice in a big bowl and sprinkle three and a half tsp of plain gelatin over it. Let the gelatin expand for about five minutes.
3. To make the other cup of juice, put the juice in a small pot and heat it. Pour the hot juice over the expanded gelatin and mix by whisking until all the gelatin is gone.
4. Put this juice mixture into the baking dish and refrigerate it for about 30 minutes.
5. While you wait, get ready for the next layer. While the first layer is cooling on the baking sheet, start the next layer. This way, the second layer will be ready to pour on top of the first layer that is already set. The cold layer will melt if the juice mix is too hot, and the colors may mix. It's also important not to mix them too early, or the juice will start to set.
6. I made one can of sweetened condensed milk for the white layer, spread it out among the layers, and then finished it with another half-can of sweetened condensed milk so it wouldn't sit while the other layers chilled in the fridge.
7. Half a cup of water and five tsp of plain gelatin should be mixed and left alone for five minutes to bloom.
8. Bring 1 3/4 cups of water to a boil. After 5 minutes of blooming, mix the gelatin, one can of sweetened condensed milk, and 1 3/4 cups of hot water with a whisk. Mixing dissolves all the gelatin.
9. Let the first layer of juice cool for 30 minutes. Then, carefully pour 1 1/2 cups of the milk mixture on top of it.
10. Do it again, switching between a rainbow-colored and a white layer to make the other layers of juice. After using up all the white mixture, make another half-batch.
11. First, dissolve 2 1/2 tsp of plain gelatin in 1/4 cup water. Then, mix 1/2 can of sweetened condensed milk and 3/4 cup of hot water using a whisk.
12. The Layered Rainbow Jello should be kept in the fridge until you're ready to serve it.

104. UBE HALAYA GELATIN

Prep Time: 15 Minutes | Cook Time: 1 Hour 15 Minutes | Total Time: 1 Hour 30 Minutes | Serving: 48

Ingredients

- 2.2 pound ube or purple yam
- ½ cup of packed brown sugar
- ½ tsp salt
- ¼ cup of unsalted butter
- 1 10- ounce can condensed milk
- 1 12- ounce can evaporated milk

Instructions

1. Cut ube or fresh yams into pieces to make room in your pot. Bring your pot to a boil and add enough water to cover everything. It takes about 30 minutes of cooking until a fork easily slides through the ube.
2. After you fish the yams out, let them cool for about 10 minutes. Mash them with a fork or potato masher while they are still warm.
3. Mix and stir 1 can of evaporated milk and ½ cup of brown sugar in a large nonstick pan or wok over medium-low heat until the sugar is gone. Add mashed yams, one can of condensed milk, and half a tsp of salt.
4. Mix the halaya until it gets very thick. The halaya will burn if you don't stir it all the time. Also, don't turn the heat up super high. At most, you should go with medium heat. It works best to go slow and steady.
5. The jam should thicken around 20 minutes into the cooking time. Add the butter and stir it until it melts and is mixed in.
6. If you can drag your spoon down the middle of the pan and the jam doesn't move, your corn is done (about 30 minutes).
7. Put in a jar that can handle heat, let it cool, and then enjoy!

105. BUKO SALAD GELATIN

Prep Time: 10 Minutes | Cook Time: 10 Minutes

Total Time: 20 Minutes | Serving: 8

Ingredients

- 4 cups of coconut juice
- 1 package agar-agar bars
- 2 cups of sugar
- 1 cup of young coconut
- 2 ½ cups of coconut milk
- 3 drops buko pandan flavor extract

Instructions

1. Cut the agar bars into little bits.
2. Soak the agar in coconut juice in a big pot for about 30 minutes or until it becomes soft.
3. Bring to a boil over medium heat and stir until the agar-agar melts.
4. After adding the sugar, stir the food often and cook for another 10 to 15 minutes.
5. Pandan flavor, coconut milk, and chopped young coconut should all be added. Stir it to ensure the color is spread out.
6. Bring to a simmer, but DO NOT BOIL. Continue cooking for two to three minutes until everything is hot.
7. Take the liquid off the heat and put it in an 8- cup of gelatin form that has been lightly greased. As it cools, the gelatin will start to set.
8. Put it in the fridge for about an hour or two or until it's completely set.
9. Carefully flip the dish onto a serving plate and cut it into serving sizes.

106. LYCHEE MANGO JELLO

Prep Time: 4 Hours 30 Minutes | Total Time: 4 Hours 30 Minutes | Serving: 6

Ingredients

- 2 packets unflavored gelatin
- 1 can lychees
- 1/2 cup of sugar
- 1/2 cup of Mango Nectar

Instructions

1. Mix mango juice and lychee drink.
2. Sprinkle 1/4 cup of juice over the gelatin in a small bowl. Let it sit for two to three minutes to soften.
3. While that happens, melt the sugar in a small pot over medium-high heat with the remaining 1/4 cup of juice. Remove the pot from the heat and stir in the softened gelatin until it dissolves. Then add the last 1 1/2 cups of juice and stir again.
4. Put the lychees in a 4-by-8-inch (6-cup) loaf pan. Pour the gelatin mixture over the lychees and gently press them down to cover them fully.
5. Put in the fridge for at least 4 hours or until firm.
6. Run hot water over the bottom of the pan for about 5 seconds to remove it. Flip it over onto a serving plate and give it a good shake to loosen up. Cut to serve.

OTHERS DESSERTS

107. KALAMAY (STICKY RICE AND COCONUT DESSERT)

Prep Time: 10 Minutes | Cook Time: 50 Minutes

Total Time: 1 Hour | Serving: 3

Ingredients

- 1/2 cup of latik
- 2 cups of coconut milk
- 2 1/4 cups of glutinous rice flour
- 2 1/4 cups of muscovado or brown sugar
- 2 cups of coconut cream
- 1/2 cup of water

Instructions

1. Set the kalamay on a plate or round pan. Place a clean banana leaf on top of the round pan. Apply coconut oil or cooking oil to the banana leaf. Save for later.
2. Mix coconut milk, coconut cream, water, and sticky rice flour in a deep pot. Mix the ingredients well until they become soft. If necessary, use a wire whisk.
3. Set the temperature to medium. Stir the mixture slowly until it gets warm. Although lumps will appear, keep stirring until bubbles appear.
4. Turn the heat down to medium heat. Stir the mixture for another 15 minutes.
5. Add the sugar. Combine well. For 30 to 40 minutes, keep mixing until the mixture becomes thick and turns dark brown.
6. Put the thick mixture on the plate or pan that has been prepared. Layer and cover with latik.
7. Let it cool for a few minutes. Serve and enjoy!

108. BUCHI (SESAME SEED BALLS)

Prep Time: 30 Minutes | Cook Time: 30 Minutes

Total Time: 1 Hour | Serving: 16

Ingredients

- ½ cup of Sweet Red Munggo Paste
- 1 ½ cups of glutinous rice flour
- ½ cup of sesame seeds
- ¾ cup of warm water
- ⅛ tsp salt
- ¼ cup of brown sugar
- ½ cup of Ube Halaya
- ¼ cup of mashed potato flakes (optional)

Instructions

1. Mix the sugar and salt with the warm water in a small bowl.
2. Mix the potato flakes and glutinous rice flour in a larger bowl. Then, mix the sugar and water until it forms a dough. You may need to add more rice flour or water for consistency. It needs to be soft and a little wet but not sticky.
3. Make little balls out of this dough about 1 ½ inches across.
4. Use both hands to press each ball flat. At this point, the dough should be smooth and without big cracks around the edges.
5. In the middle, put about a half tsp of filling. Then, gather the sides to cover the filling. Roll the ball around in your hands again to make it round and smooth.
6. After all the balls are full, sesame seeds should be added. Spread out enough sesame seeds on a flat area. Add a few drops of water to your hands and rub them together. Roll a ball around in your hands a few times. Sesame seeds should be lightly pressed into the ball as it is rolled.
7. Set oil on medium heat in a pot or deep pan. Ensure the oil is deep enough to cover the balls completely while cooking. Put enough balls in the hot oil so they don't touch each other. Fry each group for 6 to 8 minutes or until the balls turn golden brown and float to the top. Use a wire rack to drain.
8. Serve while it's still warm.

109. PANDESAL BREAD PUDDING

Prep Time: 10 Minutes | Cook Time: 45 Minutes

Total Time: 55 Minutes | Serving: 9

Ingredients

- 1 Ripe Banana
- 2 Pieces Polvoron
- 9 Mini Pandesal or 6 regular size
- Coco Jam for garnish
- ½ cup of Yema Spread
- 2 cups of Milk
- ½ cup of Langka Jam
- 4 Eggs

Instructions

Prepare the Bread:

1. Spread langka jam on one side of each piece of bread and Yema on the other. Do this again for each pandesal. Don't worry; we'll use up the jam and spread that you have left over.
2. Put the bread back together when you are done.
3. Spread 2 tbsp of butter all over your 8x8 baking dish.
4. Once the pandesal is ready, cut it into six small cubes and toss them all in the buttered baking dish.

Make the Custard:

1. Add one mashed banana and whisk the four eggs until they are foamy. Mix it again.
2. You will most likely have some leftover Yema spread. Add that and 2 cups of milk to the egg mixture. Mix well.
3. Cover the pandesal pieces in the baking dish with the custard.
4. Let the custard soak into the bread while you heat the oven to 350F.
5. Sprinkle any extra langka jam and butter around the pudding while the oven prepares to bake.
6. Also, now is a great time to crush 2 Mango Float Polvoron and sprinkle them all over the Pandesal Bread Pudding.

Bake the Pandesal Bread Pudding:

1. Bake for 40-50 minutes until the top is golden brown and crunchy and the custard has set.
2. Take out of the oven and leave to set for 10 minutes before serving.
3. To Serve:
4. Cut into 9 portions and drizzle each portion with coco jam. Best eaten on the day it was baked.

110. PUTO MAYA (STICKY RICE WITH GINGER)

Cook Time: 1 Hour 30 Minutes | Total Time: 1 Hour 30 Minutes | Serving: 8

Ingredients

- 2 quarts water
- 3 cups of sweet rice /glutinous rice
- 2 cups of coconut milk
- ¼ cup of sliced ginger
- ¼ cup of black sticky rice
- ¼ cup of brown sugar
- ½ tsp salt

Instructions

1. Soak black sticky rice in water overnight to soften the grains and cook it faster. Then, make this tasty rice dish. If you don't have time to soak the black rice beforehand, boil it in 2 cups of water and let it cook on low heat for 30 minutes.
2. When it's done, rinse the black rice with cold water to remove most of the purple color. Do the same with the white sticky rice to remove dirt. Mix the two kinds of rice in a bowl.
3. Next, peel the ginger and cut it into thin strips.
4. Add water to the bottom of your steamer and put the steamer basket on top. Ensure the basket has small holes so the rice doesn't fall out. Put banana leaves or cheesecloth inside the basket if your steamer has bigger holes.
5. Put the rice and ginger slices in the steamer. Use a spatula or spoon to spread them out evenly. Set the heat to high and cover the steamer. The water will start to boil. After the water starts to boil, turn the heat to medium-low and stir the rice every 10 minutes for 45 minutes.
6. While that's going on, mix the salt, sugar, and coconut milk in a bowl.
7. After the first 45 minutes of boiling, add the coconut milk mixture and stir it well to spread it evenly. The rice might not be fully cooked at this point. Check the black rice grains to see if they are still hard. Keep cooking if the white rice grains still look milky and feel nutty.
8. The rice should be cooked all through, soft to the bite, but not mushy. Cover the steamer and cook for another 30 minutes, turning the rice every 10 minutes until it is al dente.
9. Pair the steamed rice with hot chocolate, ripe mango, or salty dried fish for a classic and tasty meal.

111. GINATAAN HALO-HALO (COCONUT MILK AND SWEET POTATO DESSERT)

Prep Time: 5 Minutes | Cook Time: 25 Minutes | Total Time: 30 Minutes | Serving: 6

Ingredients

- 1 cup of water
- 1 1/4 cup of saging na saba
- 1/2 cup of gabi
- 4 cups of coconut milk
- 1/2 cups of sweet potato
- 1 cup of granulated white sugar
- 1/2 cup of ripe langka
- 2 cups of small sago
- 20 pieces of bilo-bilo

Instructions

1. Put water in a big pot and turn on the heat.
2. Bring to a boil. Wait until it boils again, then add 2 cups of coconut milk.
3. Put in sweet potato. Put in the gabi and cook for six minutes.
4. Add the rest of the sugar, coconut milk, and sticky rice balls, and then stir them together.
5. Let it cook for 8 minutes.
6. After you add the saging na saba, cook for three more minutes.
7. Keep cooking for three more minutes after you add the Langka.
8. Add the cooked sago slowly and stir it in.
9. After one minute, turn off the heat.
10. Warm up and serve.

112. UBE KALAMAY (PURPLE YAM STICKY RICE CAKE)

Prep Time: 10 Minutes | Cook Time: 1 Hour | Total Time: 1 Hour 10 Minutes | Serving: 6

Ingredients

- 1 ½ cup of granulated white sugar
- 3/4 cup of purple yam ube
- 2 tbsp coconut oil
- 2 tsp purple ube flavoring
- ½ cup of latik
- 4 cups of coconut milk
- 2 cups of glutinous rice flour

Instructions

1. Mix water, sticky rice flour, and 2 cups of coconut milk in a bowl. Use a wire whisk to mix well. Put away.
2. Warm up a pot. Put in two cups of coconut milk. Bring to a boil.
3. Shred the purple yam. For three minutes, stir and cook on medium heat.
4. Put the sticky rice flour mix into the pot that is cooking. Stir the items together until they are well mixed.
5. Add the sugar slowly while stirring. Keep cooking until the mixture gets thick.
6. Brush coconut oil into a mold. Fill the pan with the cooked ube kalamay and cover the shape. Use the rest of the coconut oil to cover the ube kalamay. Use a spoon to flatten the top. Latik on top.
7. Take an hour to let the kalamay cool down. Serve and enjoy!

113. KALAMAY-HATI (RICE CAKE WITH COCONUT CREAM)

Prep Time: 15 Minutes | Cook Time: 1 Hour

Total Time: 1 Hour 15 Minutes | Serving: 6

Ingredients

- 2-½ cups of muscovado brown sugar
- 2 cans coconut milk
- 2 cups of glutinous rice flour

For the Latik:

- 1 cup of coconut cream

Instructions

1. Put banana leaves wilted around the edges of a serving pan. Then, brush the leaves with coconut oil from the latik.
2. Combine coconut milk and sticky rice flour in a large nonstick pan. Whisk until smooth and free of lumps.
3. Cook over medium heat, stirring often, for 10 to 15 minutes or until the liquid thickens and turns into a smooth dough.
4. Add the muscovado brown sugar and stir until the sugar is completely melted and the mixture is uniformly brown.
5. Keep cooking for another 50 minutes to an hour or until the mixture is thick, sticky, and hard to remove from the pan.
6. Put the kalamay mixture in the pan that has been made. To spread the mixture, tap the pan gently on the counter. Apply a little oil to the knife and smooth the top.
7. Spread coconut oil on the surface and then put latik on top.

For the Latik:

1. Put the coconut cream in a pan and set it on medium heat. Stir the food occasionally as it cooks until the liquid begins to thicken.
2. Turn down the heat and keep cooking.
3. As the oil separates and lumps form, stir and scrape the sides and bottom of the pan often to prevent burning.
4. Stir and cook some more until the curds turn golden brown.
5. Put the latik in a jar and drain the oil. When you're ready, you can use it.
6. Put banana leaves around the edges of a wide serving dish and brush them with coconut oil.

114. LECHE PUTO (FLAN WITH RICE CAKE)

Prep Time: 10 Minutes | Cook Time: 10 Minutes

Total Time: 20 Minutes | Serving: 12

Ingredients

For the Flan:

- 1 can sweetened condensed milk
- 4 egg yolks
- 2 tsp lemon/calamansi juice

For the Puto:

- ½ tsp salt
- 4 egg whites
- 1¼ cups of water
- ⅔ cup of white granulated sugar
- 2 cups of self-raising flour
- 1½ tsp baking powder
- A few drops of yellow liquid food coloring (optional)

Instructions

Prepare the Flan:

1. Mix the egg whites and sweetened condensed milk in a small bowl. Add lemon juice or flavor.
2. Use a plastic sauce dispenser for easy filling.
3. Heat Steamer:
4. Bring water to a boil in the steamer's bottom pan. Wrap a towel around the steamer cover.

Prepare Moulds:

1. Grease puto moulds.
2. Use about ⅓ of the flan mixture to fill each mold.
3. Turn the heat down to low and steam the flan for five to seven minutes, or until it's not liquid but also not set. Let cool down.

Prepare the Puto Mixture:

1. Sift together the self-raising flour, baking powder, sugar, and salt in a medium bowl.
2. Add the egg whites and water and mix just until they are mixed. Do not mix too much. Move to a container made of plastic.

Steam the Puto:

1. Heat the steamer again. Add more water if you need to, and boil it quickly.
2. Pour the puto mixture slowly into the molds until they are almost full. Pour it over the cold flan.
3. For another 10 minutes, steam on low heat.

Cool and Remove:

1. To cool down a bit, take it out of the steamer.
2. Slip the mold upside down and tap it to release the leche puto. To remove it, carefully run a small knife around the puto layer only.

115. NILUPAK (MASHED ROOT CROP WITH BUTTER AND CHEESE)

Prep Time: 10 Minutes | Cook Time: 40 Minutes

Total Time: 50 Minutes | Serving: 8

Ingredients

- ½ cup of butter
- water
- 2 pounds cassava
- 1 tbsp salt
- 1 cup of sweetened condensed milk
- 1 cup of American processed cheese

Instructions

1. Use melted butter or margarine to coat the sides and bottom of a baking dish. Set the dish aside.
2. Put cassava, salt, and enough water to cover it in a pot over medium-low heat. Bring to a boil, then cover and cook for 20 minutes or until very soft. Remove the cassava from the liquid and let it cool.
3. Remove the tough, stringy center and throw it away. Mash the boiling cassava until there are no more lumps. You can use a mortar and pestle or a potato masher for this.
4. Mix about 4 cups of cassava with butter, condensed milk, and salt in a bowl. Stir slowly until smooth and creamy.
5. Put the mixture into the prepared baking dish and spread it out evenly with a spoon. Run the tines of a fork over the surface to make pretty lines.
6. Spread softened butter on top, if desired. Sprinkle top with shredded cheese and cut into servings.

Printed in Great Britain
by Amazon